"The beauty of Africa comes from the richness of its linguistic and cultural diversity, like an exquisite multi-coloured carpet".

Rufin Batota-Mpeho

Morphosyntax of the verb in Lingala

A generative approach

Rufin Batota-Mpeho, MA
Researcher in General and
African Linguistics

Editor:	Lulu publishing
Publisher:	Rufin Batota-Mpeho
Copyright Year:	© 2012
Country:	United Kingdom
Edition:	First edition

ISBN: 978-1-291-23617-0

TABLE OF CONTENTS

ACKNOWLEDGEMENT

I am immensely grateful to Dr Marten Lutz - Professor of African and General Linguistics at School of Oriental and African Studies (SOAS), University of London - whose insightful comments helped to me improve this work.

Heartfelt thanks to Dr Philippe Samba-Samba - Lecturer of Bantu and General Linguistics at Marien Ngouabi University, Congo - whose lectures in Bantu Linguistics were of great help to write this paper.

I would like to thank my tutors at London Meridian College, namely Susan Haque and David Page, whose lectures in General English enthused me to substantially improve my speaking and writing abilities.

ABBREVIATIONS

A: Aspect
AUX: Auxiliary
APPL: Applicative
ASS: Associative
BEN: Beneficiary
CAUS: Causative
DEM: Demonstrative
Ditrans: Di-transitive
ECM: Exceptional case marking
EXT: Extension
(*ei*) or (i): Trace
FPCs: Feature Percolation Conventions
FUT: Future
FV: Final vowel
HAB: Habitual
INF: Infinitive
INTRANS: Intransitive
L-s: Logico-semantic
N: Noun
Ncl: Noun Class
NP: Noun phrase
NTS: N-Tier Structure
OBJ: Object
PAST: Past
PP: Past participle
PERF: Perfective
PP: Prepositional Phrase
PRES: Present
PRN: Pronoun
PRG: Progressive
REV: Reversive
RECPR: Reciprocal
REL: Relarive pronoun
REFL: Reflexive

RES: Resultative
SM: Subject marker
SUB: Subject
TRANS: Transitive
STAT: Stative
T: Tense
TA: Tense and Aspect
TS: Tense Suffix
V': Extended Verb
VB: Verbal base
VP: Verb phrase
VS: Verb stem
Vu: Verb unit
Vu': Extended verb unit

SYMBOLS

/ / Phonemic slashes

[ ] Semantic features

/ In the environment of

__ Place of occurrence

' ' Gloss of meaning

⇒ Continuation rule

↪ Percolation arrow

-------- Tier mapping

( ) Gloss in English

ABSTRACT

This paper is aimed at scrutinising the morphosyntax of the verb in Lingala. The verb in Bantu languages is usually referred to as the verb unit as it is a concatenation of different morphemes. It is a self- contained unit in that it has not only the verb root as the core or central element, but it also encodes information about grammatical functions (e.g. subject, direct object and oblique object, polarity, tense, etc.). Dealing with the highly agglutinative verb unit in the framework of generative grammar constitutes the uniqueness of this paper.

To begin with, the internal structure of the verb unit is analysed, modelling myself on Meeussen's (1967) Bantu verb unit structure. Lingala verb unit is composed of a pre-stem, a stem and what I call a post-stem. Each component of the unit is thoroughly anatomised.

Then, verb extensions are analysed in the light of generative morphology using Lieber's (1980, 1983) Morphological Sub-categorisation Frames and Feature Percolation Conventions (FPCs). The causative, passive, applicative and reflexive extensions, which reduce or increase the valence of the verb, are illustrated in the framework of Government-Binding syntax, having recourse to Marantz's (1984) “merger” and Baker's (1988) “incorporation” theories.

Finally, as a contribution to morphological valence changing, I have developed the N-Tier Structure (NTS) theory. It is an “all-in-one” tree structure with distinct layers displaying syntactic, morphological, lexical and sometimes phonological information of sentences before and after the valence alteration. To test its universality, The NTS theory has been applied to English passive and word formation.

DATA COLLECTION

As a mature speaker of Lingala as a second language, I have played an effective role as self-informant, as Lyon (1968) concedes that a linguist may of course be his own informant if he is describing his own language.

However, my data have been submitted to other speakers to verify or test what Lyon (1968) calls their 'acceptability':
In the case the linguist is his own informant, Lyon claims that he must be on his guard against the danger of producing for description a corpus of materials which includes only such sentences as to satisfy his preconceived ideas about the language. As the description proceeds the linguist can obtain further utterances of various kinds from his informants, so as to extend the corpus and he can check with the *acceptability* of sentences which he himself constructs in order to test the generality of his tentative rules.

I have been helped by members of my micro-speech community to collect data and verify their acceptability. My main informants were chosen due to their being literate and natively able to speak and write Lingala.

Furthermore, Lingala has a wide range of written literature, including academic books, fiction, translated Bible, dictionaries and online materials, which have also been a wealthy source of data collection.

CHAPTER I: LINGUISTIC OVERVIEW

1.1- Localisation

According to Wikipedia,

"Lingala is a Bantu language spoken throughout the Northwest of the Democratic Republic of Congo (Congo-Kinshasa) and the large part of the Republic of Congo (Congo-Brazzaville), as well as to some degree in Angola and African Central Republic. It has over 10 millions speakers". (en.wikipedia.org/Lingala Language). Being one of the national languages in both Congo, Lingala is in fact spoken by more than 10 million. Over 90% of the population in Democratic Republic of Congo and at least 50% of in Republic of Congo speak Lingala as second language.

1.2. History

The origin of Lingala is very controversial due to the diversity of versions. However, the common point is that Lingala originated from Bobangi, spoken alongside the Congo River, which functioned as the language of trade among the riverside villages. When the colonists (France and Belgium) penetrated both sides of the Congo River, Lingala came into wider use for missionary and administrative purposes. It became the common vernacular.

Gruyter (1989) explains that:

"The origin of Lingala illustrates the way a number of different forces interact in the life of a language in the modern political state. Although its history parallels in some way that of other national languages of the world, it stands apart in one important respect... It does not owe its existence to a particular natural speech community whose language was adopted by others as second language... Its speakers came into existence at the same time that it became a linguistic reality. The language and the speech community evolved together" (P.388).

In Congo-Brazzaville, Lingala and Kituba are the two national languages, used in the media and as vernacular languages. Lingala is mainly used in the Centre and North part of the country (by Teke and Mbochi linguistic groups) while Kituba is used in the South (mainly by the Kongo linguistic group). In Brazzaville, the capital city, Lingala is mostly spoken in the north districts where the majority of inhabitants belong to Teke and Mbochi groups. Although Kituba is the vernacular in the south part of Brazzaville, Kilaadi is also used, mainly in the south-west, where most of the population come from the region of Pool in the south of Republic of Congo.

1.3. Classification

According to the general classification of Bantu Languages, Lingala is classed as follows:

Table1.1

-Phylum:	Niger-kordofanian
-Sub-phylum:	Niger-Congo
-Family:	Benue-Congo
-Sub-family:	Bantoid
-Branch:	Bantu
-Zone:	C
-Group:	C40 (SIL) / C36D (Guthrie)

Malcom Guthrie's classification and coding system is undoubtedly the most well-known, although many other studies have been undertaken during the twentieth century. Most of his detractors think that Guthrie's encoding system is widely used as a referential tool when talking of individual languages, but not successful as linguistic-genetic statement.

1.4. Phonology

This summarises the basic phonology of Lingala including consonants, pre-nasalised consonants, the vowel system, phonotactics and tone.

1.4.1. Consonants

Table 1.2

	Labial	Alveolar	Post-alveolar	Labio-velar	Velar
Nasal	m	n			ŋ
Plosive	p b	t d			k g
Fricative	f v	s z	r		
Approx		l	j	w	

1.4.2. Pre-nasalised consonants

Some consonants can be preceded by a nasal. This depends on nasal harmony:

Labio-plosive/fricative consonants are preceded by labio-nasal /***m*** /

(1.1)
/mp/ /mpuku/ 'rat'
/mb/ /mbula/ 'rain'

Alveo-plosive/fricative are preceded by alveo-nasal ***/n/***

(1.2)
/nt/ /ntaba/ 'lamb'
/nd/ /ndumba/ 'prostitute'
/nz/ /nzala/ 'hunger'

Velar-plosive are preceded by velar-nasal /***ŋ*** /
(1.3)
/ŋk/ /ŋkema/ 'monkey'
/ŋg/ /ŋgɔlɔ / 'catfish'

1.4.3 Vowels

Table 1.3

	Front	Back
close	i	u
mid-close	e	o
mid-open	ɛ	ɔ
open	a	

1.4.4. Phonotactics

Phonotactics regulates the way lower units (C and V) of the phonological hierarchy can combine. Lingala is a language of the type CV and V. It permits consonant cluster *C only in syllable initial position. Following are the permissible sequences of phonemes.

a) The minimum syllable: V

A minimum syllable comprises only a peak. They include the 2sg pronoun ***o*-,** the 3sg pronouns ***a*-** and ***e*-** (cf. Table 2.2) and the noun class7 ***e*-** (cf.chap 2.6)

(1.4)
e-lamba 'cloth'
7-cloth

(1.5)
a- lal- i 'she has slept'
3sg-sleep-ts

b) The CV syllable: CV

This is the basic or canonical structure:

(1.6)
libala 'marriage'
cvcvcv

c) The CCV syllable

The cluster CC includes the pre-nasalised consonants

(1.7)
/mpuku/ 'mouse/rat'
ccvcv

/mbɔŋgɔ / 'money'
ccvccv

d) The CCCV syllable

The CCC is mainly a pre-nasalised followed by a glide:

(1.8)
/mbwa/ 'dog'
cccv

/mpjodi/ ' mackerel'
cccv

Words borrowed from English or French have been adapted to the syllable cluster of Lingala:

(1.9)
milk ⟹ /miliki/
cvcc cvcvcv

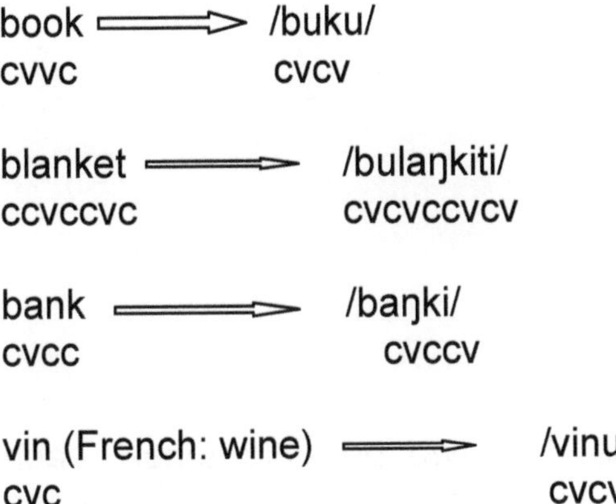

Many other words were borrowed from Portugese such as:

(1.10)
Mesa: table
Sapatu: shoes
Manteka: butter

1.4.5. Length formation

When two similar vowels occur in immediate environment, their coalition derives a similar long vowel, as in the example below:

(1.11) ba -ana ⟹ /ba:na/
2-child children

1.4.6. Glide formation

The combination of some vowels results in glide formation, mainly when a noun class is followed by noun stem starting with a vowel, as in (1.12) below:

(1.12)
/u/+/a/=/wa/
mu -ana = /mwana/
1-child

/u/+/i/=/wi/
mo-yindo=/mwi:ndo/
1-black

/u/+/e/=/we/
mu-ela=/mwela/
1-disabled'

1.4.7. Tone

Lingala, a tonal language, has two possible tones: each vowel bears a tone either a low (normal) or high. Tone can also bear a lexical or grammatical meaning.

(1.13)
motó 'head'
móto 'fire'

na-zal-á 'I was' (Past)
ná-zal-a 'I be' (Subjunctive)

1.5. Summary

Lingala is a result of language contact. Spoken in Congo-Brazzaville, Congo-Kinshasa and to some extent in Angola and Central African Republic, it has been classified in Bantu as C36D by Guthrie. It has six vowels and seventeen consonants. Its tone is either low or high and plays a lexical and syntactic role. Having a basic CV and V cluster, Lingala has borrowed many words from Portuguese, French and English that have been adapted to its syllable structure.

CHAPTER II: STRUCTURE OF THE VERB UNIT

Introduction

This chapter aims at analysing the structure of the verb unit in Lingala. After reviewing Meeussen's structure and proposing one that applies in Lingala, the different elements the verb unit are scrutinised: the verbal stem, pronominal clitics, extensions, tense and aspect. Furthermore, Lieber's Morphological Subcategorisation Framework and Feature Percolation Conventions are used to deal the verb structure

2.1- Meeussen's Bantu structure (1967)

Meeussen (1967) proposed the following structure of the verb unit in Bantu Languages:

(2.1)

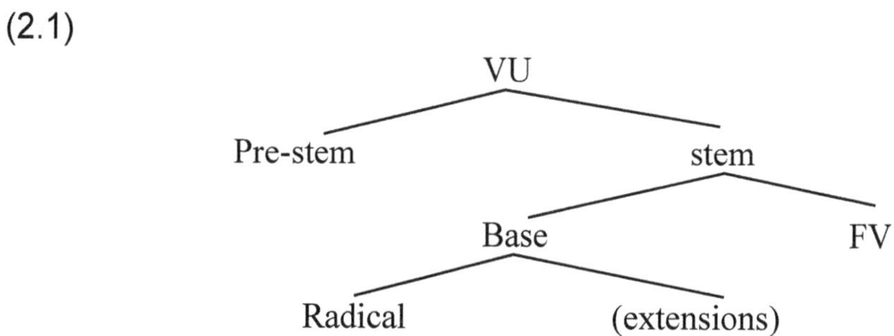

The verbal base is made of the root plus extensions (VB=Root + Extensions), while the verbal stem is composed of the verbal base plus the final vowel (Verbal stem=Root + extension + final vowel).

2.2. Proposed Lingala structure

The structure (2.1) can be partially applied in Lingala, where other affixes expressing tense and aspect may occur between extensions and the FV. In this case, all affixes coming after extensions (including the FV) are not part of the stem, but constitute what I have called 'post-stem'. Following my analysis, I propose the following tree structure.

(2.2)

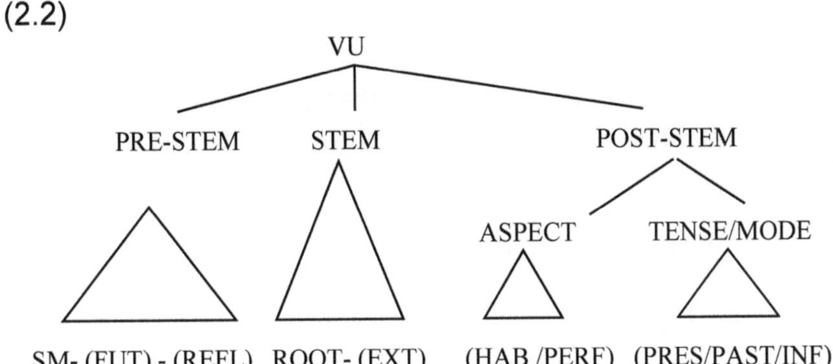

VU= PRE-STEM + STEM+ POST-STEM
PRE-STEM= SM-(FUT)-(REFL)
STEM= BASE
BASE= ROOT-(EXT)
POST-STEM= ASPECT-TENSE/MODE (TM)
ASPECT= HAB / PERF
TENSE/MODE = PRES / PAST/INF

2.3. The Verbal stem

The verbal stem is simply reduced to verbal base, made of the root and extensions..

2.3.1. The Root

The root is the nucleus of the verb unit. Let us first analyse the infinitive verb **kobala** "to get married" in (2.3):

(2.3)

ko – ***bal*** – a
INF-***Root***-FV

The prefix **ko**- and the final vowel **-a** are simultaneously attached to the root to form the infinitive. I consider them as a kind of discontinuous affix, a *circumfix*.

2.3.1.1. Root alteration

Most of verb roots are regular in that they do not change in any circumstances. Following are some exceptions:
(2.4)

ko-***kend***-a "to go"
na-***key***-i "I am gone"

ko-***li***-a "to eat"
na-***ley***-i " I have eaten"

ko-***w***-a "to die"
a-***wey***-i "He is dead"

2.3.1.2. Vowel harmony

When there is a mid-open vowel is used in the verb root, it harmonises with the vowels in the prefix and suffix:

(2.5)a		(2.5)b	
ko-sek-a	or	kɔ-sɛk-ɛ	"to laugh"
ko-lemb-a		kɔ-lɛmb-ɛ	"to get tired"
ko-kend-a		kɔ-kɛnd-ɛ	"to leave, go"
ko-kond-a		kɔ-kɔnd-ɔ	"to lose weight"

Using mid-open vowels, as in (2.5) b, is a case of free variation.

2.3.2. Extensions

Extensions comprise the causative, applicative, reversive, passive, reciprocal and positional.

2.3.2.1 Causative: -is

It adds the idea of "to cause to do" the action of the main verb:

(2.6)

ko-bin-a	"to dance"
ko-bin-***is***-a	"to cause to dance"
ko-kom-a	"to write"
ko-kom-***is***-a	"to cause to write"

2.3.2.2- Applicative/benefactive: -el

It applies the action to an expressed object and is usually translated by the preposition "for" in English. It is commonly called the "prepositional" extension.

(2.7)

ko-kom-a	"to write"
ko-kom-***el***-a	"to write for/to"
ko-lam-ba	"to cook"
ko-lamb-***el***-a	"to cook for"

2.3.2.3- Reversive: -ol-

It gives the opposite meaning of the "simplex" verb, rather like the prefix ***un-*** in English.

(2.8)

ko-pik-a	"to stake down"
ko-pik-***ol***-a	"to uproot"
ko-kund-a	"to bury"
ko kund-***ol***-a	"to unearth"
ko-kang-a	"to tie"
ko-kang-***ol***-a	"to untie"

2.3.2.4- Passive: -am

It is used to transform a verb into passive voice.

(2.9)

ko-bot-a	"to give birth"
ko-bot-***am***-a	"to be born"
ko-bet-a	"to beat"
ko-bet-***am***-a	"to be beaten"

2.3.2.5- Positional: -am/-em

It expresses a static position. This extension is quite different from the passive one.

(2.10)

*ko-tel-***em***-a	"to stand up"
*ko-bat-***am***-a	"to lie down and remain quiet"
*ko-fuk-***am***-a	"to kneel down"

*The asterisk means that the "simplex" form of the verb is not attested in the language.

2.3.2.6- Associative/reciprocal:-an/-is-an

The associative ***-an-*** involves reciprocity amongst two people, while the reciprocal ***-is-an-*** includes more than two people.

(2.11

ko-bal-a	"to marry"
ko-bal-***an***-a	"to marry (each other)"
ko-bal-***is-an***-a	"to marry one another"
ko-sal-a	"to work"
ko-sal-***is-an***-a	"to help one another"

ko-ling-a "to love"
ko-ling-***an***-a "to love each other"

ko-lob-a "to speak"
ko-lob-***an***-a "to speak each other"

ko-tal-a "to see"
ko-tal-***is-an***-a "to visit one another"

2.4. Pre-stem

The pre-stem includes personal pronouns, noun classes, the reflexive affix, progressive and future morphemes

2.4.1. Subject markers

Subject markers include personal pronouns and noun classes.

2.4.1.1. Personal pronouns

There are six personal pronouns, as follows:
Table 2.2

Pronouns	Person	Number
na-	1	Sg
o-	2	Sg
a-	3Human	Sg
e-	3 animal/inanimate	Sg
to-	1	Pl
bo-	2	Pl
ba-	3	Pl

When a noun is used as subject, its co-related personal pronoun is repeated in the verb unit, as in the following examples:

(2.12)
Mama ***a***-lal-í
Mum ***she***- sleep-TS
(Mum has slept)

Mbwa ***e***-lal-í
Dog ***it***-sleep-TS
(The dog has slept)

2.4.1.2. Noun classes

Lingala has the following noun class:
(2.13)

1.mo/mu-	mo-to (person)
2.ba-	ba-to (people)
3.mo-	mo-kila (tail)
4.mi-	mi-kila (tails)
5.li-	li-bala (marriage)
6.ma-	ma-bala (marriages)
7.e-	e-lamba (cloth)
8.bi-	bi-lamba (clothes)
9. m-/n-	ntaba (goat)
10. m-/n-	ntaba (goats)
9a.	sanza (sun)
10a.	sanza (suns)
11. lo-	lo-lemo (tongue)
12. bo	bo-soto (dirt)

Noun classes are co-indexed in the verb unit:

(2.14)
Ba-na ***ba***-lal-i
2-children **2**-sleep-TS
(Children have slept)

Li-bala ***li***-kuf-i
5-marriage **5**-die-T
(The marriage is broken)

A more detailed study is provided in 2.7.

2.4.2. Reflexive

The reflexive morpheme is ***-mí-***. This morphological reflexive is non- harmonic in that it does not vary according to any features of the subject argument. It is always prefixed immediately to the root.

(2.15)
a – ko – ***mí*** – tal – a
2sg-Fut-***REFL***-look-Fv
(He/she will look at him/herself)

2.4.3 Future

The future is expressed by the prefix ***-kó-*** (with a high tone). It is either directly attached to the verb root or preceded by the reflexive.

(2.16)
Na – ***kó*** – lamb - a
1sg-***FUT***-cook-FV
(I will cook)

2.4.4. Progressive

In the informal Lingala, the prefix ***-zó-*** is usually used to express an action, which takes place in the present only, as in the following examples:

(2.17)
na – ***zó*** – li - a
1sg-***PRG***-eat-FV
(I am eating)

mokonzi mo – ***zó***- bin- a
President SM-***PRG***-dance-FV
(The President is dancing)

Grammatically, the progressive is formed by conjugating the verb 'ko-zal-a' (to be) plus the infinitive of the main verb, as exemplified in (2.18) below:

(2.18)
na – zal –i ko-li-a
1sg-be-ts INF-eat-FV
(I am eating)

mokonzi mo – zal-i ko-bin-a
President SM-be-TS INF-dance-FV
(The President is dancing)

2.5. Post-stem

Tense, aspect and modality are expressed by suffixing the following extensions to the verb.

2.5.1. Perfective

The perfect extension is ***-ak-*** (with a low tone). It acts as auxiliaries "have" and "be" in English. It is immediately attached to the root or preceded by an extension.

(2.19)
na – sal – ***ak*** – á na banki
I–work- ***PERF***-TS in bank
'I had worked for a bank'

Na –lamb-el-***ak***-í bana
I-cook-Appl-***PERF***-TS children
'I have worked for the children"

2.5.2. Habitual

The habitual affix is ***-ák-***. Two aspects make it different from the perfect morpheme: it bears a high tone and is followed neither by the present nor by the past morphemes, but by the final vowel ***-a*** (with a low tone), as illustrated:

(2.20)
na-li-***ák***-a ndunda
1sg-eat-***HAB***-FV vegetables
'I usually eat vegetables'

(2.21)
na- mel – ***ák***- a vinu ***te***
1sg-drink-**HAB**-FV wine ***NEG***
'I do not to drink wine (usually)'

NB: Lingala negation is among the exceptions from the common morphological negation in Bantu Languages. It is *"a less typical type of negation expressed by a sentence-final function word"* (Tom Güldemann, 2010).

2.5.3. The final vowel

The final vowel includes the infinitive marker ***-a*** (cf chap 2.3), the present morpheme ***-í*** and the past morpheme ***-á.***

2.5.3.1. The present

The present morpheme is ***-í*** (with a high tone). It is the ultimate prefix of the verb unit. It may occur either in the immediate environment after the root, an extension or the perfect affix. Lingala present tense normally indicates that the effect of the past action continues into the present. The present progressive (2.17) is used when the action is taking place.

(2.22)
na – lamb-***í***
1sg-cook-***PRES***
(I (just) cooked)

2.5.3.2. The past

The past morpheme is ***-á*** (with a high tone). It differs from the final vowel suffix (FV) ***–a,*** which bears a low tone. It occurs in the same environment as the present morpheme.

(2.23)
na – lamb-***á***
1sg-cook-**PAST**
(I cooked)

2.5.3.3. The Infinitive marker

The infinitive marker **-a** (cf 2.3) occurs as final vowel when the verb root is prefixed by the future **-ko-** and the progressive **-zo-,** or suffixed by the habitual -**ák-.** It is also used with the subjunctive and imperative as in the following illustrations:

(2.24) **Imperative**

Φ- sál- **a**
2sg-work-INF
(work)

To- sál- **a**
1Pl-work-INF
(Let us work)

Bo- sál- **a**
2Pl-work-INF
(let you work)

There are only three persons in the imperative and the 2sg is omitted. The tone is placed on the root vowel.

Subjunctive

(2.25)

Present Subjunctive

ná-zal-a mokonzi
1sg-be-FV president
(I be president)

Perfect Subjunctive

ná-zal-ak-a mokonzi
1sg-be-PERF-FV president
(I were president)

Future Subjunctive

ná-ko-zal-a ko-zal-a mokonzi
1sg-FUT-be-FV Inf-be –FV president
(I were to be president)

In subjunctive, the high tone is located on the personal pronoun vowel.

NB: Tone plays a crucially important role in conjugation. It clearly differentiates between the imperative, the subjunctive and the past, as exemplified in (2.26):

(2.26)
Bo-s**á**l-a (Imperative)
(Let you work)

B**ó**-sal-a (Present Subjunctive)
(you worked)

Bo-sal-**á** (Past)
(you worked)

This is a very illustrative example of phonology-syntax interface in Lingala.

2.6. Examples of complex verb units

The sentences below exemplify a diversity of possible complex verb unit structures:
(2.27)
Petelo **a-ko-mi-ley-is-a**
Peter **3SM-Fut-Refl-eat-Caus-FV**
(Peter will feed himself)

(2.28)
Papa na mama **ba-zo-somb-el-a** bana bilamba
Dad and Mum **3SM-Prog-buy-Appl-FV** children clothes
(Dad and Mum are buying clothes for children)

(2.29)
Ba-na **ba-kuf-ák-a** nzala na bitumba
2-child **2SM-die-Hab-FV** hunger in wars
(Children usually starve during wars)

(2.30)
Ba-to **ba**-bale **ba-bal-an-ak-í**
2-person **2**-two **2SM-marry-Recipr-Perf-Pres**
(Two people have got married)

(2.31)
Li-ngomba **li-sal-am-ak-á** lelo mbula nzomi
5-organisation **5SM-found-Pass-Perf-Past** today years ten
(The organisation was founded ten years ago)

2.7. Noun class agreement

Apart from the verb unit, noun classes are in agreement with other parts of a sentence such as demonstratives, adjectives, quantitative, determiners and relative pronouns, as in the following sentences.

(2.32)
Li-kama **li**-nene **li**-a nzela **li**-bom-is-i bato
5-accident **5**-big **5**-of road **5SM**-kill-Caus-Pres people
(A big road accident has killed people)

(2.33)
Li-bala **li**-susu **li**-nene **li**-ko-sal-am-a
5-marriage **5**-another **5**-big **5**-Fut-Pass-FV
(Another big marriage will be celebrated)

(2.34)
Ba-na **ba**-sato, **ba-ye** **ba**-bung-ak-i **ba**-kuf-i
2-child **2**-three, **2-Rel** **2SM**-disappear-Perf-TS **2SM**-die-TS
(The three young children, who disappeared, are dead)

(2.35)
E-lamba **e**-yindo, **e-ye** **e**-somb-am-i na mama, **e**-zal-i **e**-layi
7-cloth **7**-black **7-Rel** **7**-buy-Pass-TS by Mum **7**-be-ts **7**-small
(The black dress, which is bought by Mum, is long)

NB: In sentences (2.34) and (2.35), the relative pronoun is expressed by suffixing the corresponding noun class to the word **ye**. Let us consider the complex sentence (2.36):

(2.36)
Li-kasa **li-ye** li kwey-i na nzete li-zal-i li-ke
5-leaf **5-REL** 5SM-fall-ts from tree 5-be-ts 5-small
(The leaf that has fallen from the tree is small)

The independent clause is (2.37):

(2.37)
Li-kasa li-zal-i li-ke
5-leaf 5SM-be-TS 5-small
(The leaf is small)

While the relative clause will be (2.38)

(2.38)
Li-ye li-kwey-i na nzete
5-REL 5SM-fall-ts from tree
(That has fallen from the tree)

In the spoken language, however, the relative pronoun may be omitted. In this case, the tone is gradually raised in the first clause and slowly falls in the second.

(2.39)
Increasing tone peak decreasing tone

Li-kasa li-kwey-i na nzete, li-zal-i li-ke
5-leaf 5SM-fall-TS from tree 5SM-be-TS 5-small
(The leaf that has fallen from the tree is small)

(2.39) is one of the case where phonology and syntax interface in Lingala.

Clefting and **fronting (or topicalization)** is achieved by simply changing words order in a sentence. For instance, (2.36) may be differently expressed as (2.40), (2.41) and (2.42):

(2.40)
Li-zal-i li-ke li-kasa li-ye li-kwey-i na nzete
5SM-be-TS 5-small 5-leaf 5-REL 5SM-fall-TS from tree
(It is small, the leaf that has fallen from the tree)

(2.41)
Li-ye li-zal-i li-ke li-kasa li-kwey-i na nzete
5-REL 5SM-be-TS 5-leaf 5SM-fall-TS from tree
(What is small is the leaf fallen from the tree)

(2.42)
Li-ye li-kwey-i na nzete li-zal-i li-kasa li-ke
5-REL 5-fall-ts from tree 5SM-be-ts 5-leaf 5-small
(What has fallen from the tree is the small leaf)

2.8. Reduplication

In Lingala, verbs, adjectives, nouns and pronouns may be reduplicated as a result of intensifying or altering their meaning.

2.8.1. Verb reduplication

Verb reduplication is widely used in Lingala. It either alters the primary meaning of the verb, or adds such information as adverb or preposition.

(2.43)

ko-luk-a	'to search'
ko-luk-a luk-a	'to search everywhere'
ko-bal-a	'to get married'
ko-bal-a bal-a	'to get married repeatedly'

ko-lal-a	'to sleep'
ko-lal-a lal-a	'to sleep excessively'
ko-tamb-ol-a	'to walk'
ko-tamb-ol-a tamb-ol-a	'to wander about (uselessly)'
ko-lob-a	'to speak'
ko-lob-a lob-a	'to gossip'

Sentences with verb duplication are exemplified in the following:

(2.44)
na-**tamb-ol**-i **tamb-ol**-i ko-**luk**-a **luk**-a mwana
1sg-**walk**-ts **walk**-ts inf-**search**-FV **search**-FV child
(I wander about to search for the child everywhere)

(2.45)
ko-**lob**-a **lob**-a e-zal-i mabe
Inf-**speak**-Fv **speak**-FV 3sg-be-ts bad
(Gossiping is bad)

2.8.2. Adjective reduplication

In Lingala, repeating adjectives intensifies their meaning. In this case, the second adjective acts as an adverb in English..

(2.46)
Ba-na ba-**ke** ba-**ke**
2-child 2-**small** 2-**small**
(Very young children)

(2.47)
Bi-bwele bi-**nene** bi-**nene**
8-animal 8-**big** 8-**big**
(Extremely big animals)

(2.48)
Ba-to ba-**kuse** ba-**kuse**
2-person 2-**short** 2-**short**
(Very short people)

2.8.3. Noun reduplication

Nouns can also be reduplicated; this alters the meaning of the initial word:

(2.50)
Ba-to ba-zo-wut-a bi-**sika** na bi-**sika**
2-person 2-PROG-come 8-**place** of 8-**place**
(People are coming from everywhere)

(2.51)
Ba-to ba-kut-an-i mi-**kolo** na mi-**kolo**
2-person 2-meet-ASS-ts 4-day of 4-day
(People have met for many days)

(2.52)
Bi-lia bi-a mo-**kolo** na mo-**kolo**
8-food 8-of 3-**day** of 3-**day**
(Everyday's/ daily food)

(2.53)
Lobi **lobi** o-ko-zong-a mboka
Tomorrow **tomorrow** 2sg-Fut-return-Fv country
(In the near future, you are going back home)

2.8.4. Object pronoun reduplication

Following are the object pronouns of Lingala:

(2.54)

ngayi	1sgObj	me
yo	2sgObj	you
ye	3sgObj	him, her
biso	1plrObj	us
bino	2plrObj	you
bango	3plrObj	them

Object pronouns are syntactically independent in that they are not part the verb unit, as in the provided example:

(2.55)

Mama	a-somb-el-i	**ngayi**	bilamba
Mum	3SM-buy-APPL-TS	**me**	clothes

(Mum has bought clothes for me)

The object pronoun is repeated to emphasise on the action done on oneself:

(2.56)

Ba-bom-an-i	**bango** na **bango**
They-kill-Recpr-TS	**them** and **them**

(They kill each other (among themselves))

(2.57)

To-zal-i	**biso** na **biso**
We-be-TS	**us** and **us**

(We are the same people)

Object pronouns may be occur at the beginning of the sentence. In this case, they must be followed by their corresponding subject pronoun.

(2.58)

Bino	na	**ngayi**	**to**-zal-i	ba-ndeko
You	and	**me**	**we**-be-ts	2-relative

(You and I are relatives)

(2.59)

Yo	na	**ye**	**bo**-ling-an-i	mingi
You	and	**him**	**you**-love-Recpr-ts	much

(You and he love each other very much)

2.9. Lieber's (1980,1982) theory on affixation

Lieber provided Subcategorisation Frames and Feature Percolation Conventions (FPCs) to deal with word structure in generative grammar.

2.9.1. Morphological subcategorisation frames.

Lieber assumes that all morphemes bound and free, are provided with frames which state what categories they must attach to, together with their morpho-syntactic features.
For instance, the English plural morpheme ***-s*** has the following frame:

(2.60)
-s: [[N] -] [N,+Plural] e.g. [[book]–***s***]

The feature [N,+Plural] means that the morpheme ***-s*** is suffixed to nouns to form the plural.

Modelled on Lieber, I provide frames for some Lingala verb affixes as follows:

(2.61)

-ko- :	[-[v]]	[v, +Future]
-mi- :	[- [v]]	[v,+ Reflexive]
-is- :	[[v]-]	[v, +Causative]
-am- :	[[v]-]	[v, + Passive]
-ak- :	[[v]-]	[v, +Perfect]
-ák- :	[[v]-]	[v,+Habitual]

2.9.2- Feature Percolation Conventions (FPCs)

In this theory, Lieber provides unlabelled trees to which lexical entries, stems and affixes are inserted under their terminal node. They determine the labelling of the whole tree by "percolating" their features upwards. Percolation is achieved by four conventions. To illustrate, I am going to use the first two conventions:

FPC I: Features of a stem are passed to the first dominating non-banching node.

FPCII: Affixes features are passed to the first dominating nodes, which branches.

Let us first exemplify FPC I and FPC II with the plural noun "books":

a) Unlabelled tree

b) Morphemes and features insertion

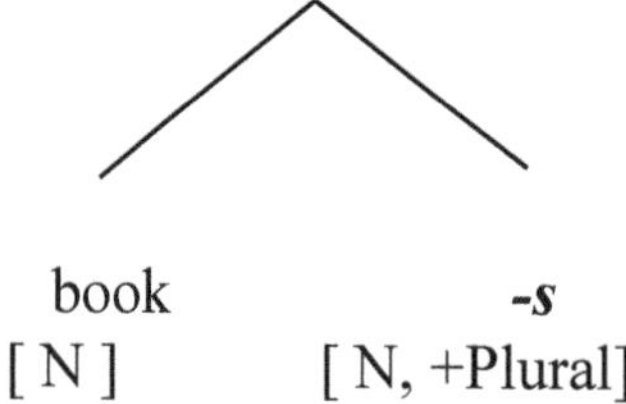

c) FPC I

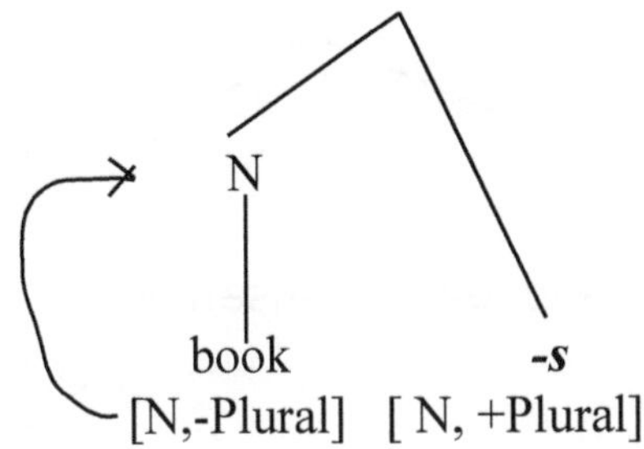

d) FPC II

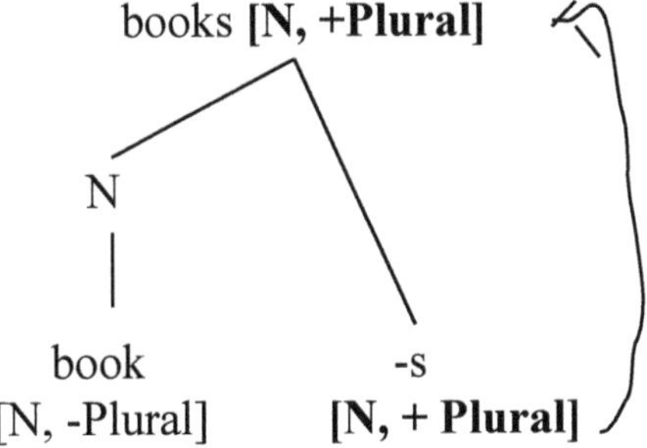

FPCs can be applied to highly morphological Bantu languages like Lingala. I would like to exemplify the FPCs with the reflexive and the causative affixes.

Let me first consider the reflexive verb in the sentence (2.61):
(2.62)
Moyibi mo-***mi-bom***-i
3-burglar SM-***REFL-kill***-TS
'The burglar has killed himself'

(2.63) Morpho-syntactic features of the reflexive verb base:

-***mi***- “oneself” [V, +Reflexive]
-***bom***- “kill” [V, +Root]

a) Unlabelled tree

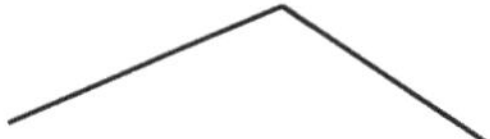

b) Morphemes and features insertion

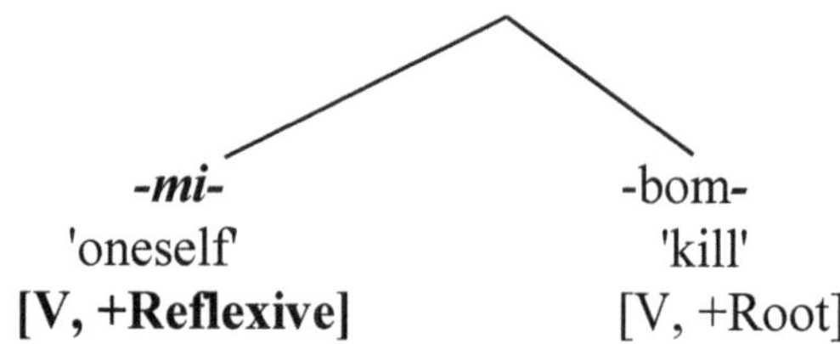

c) FPC I

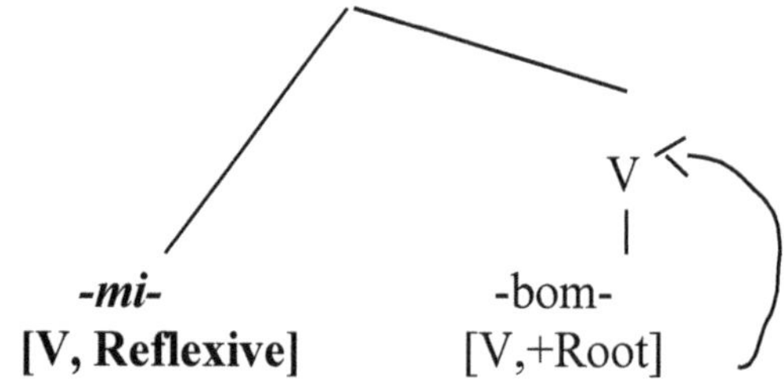

d) FPC II

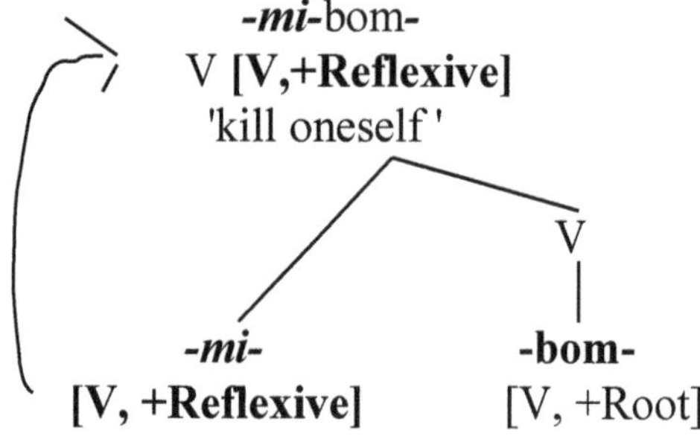

The second illustration is the causative verb in the sentence below:

(2.64)
mwana a – ***bom – is*** – i mbwa
1-child SM- ***kill-CAUS-***TS dog
'The child has caused the dog die'

(2.65) Morpho-syntactic features of the causative verb base
-bom- [V,+Root]
-***is-*** [V, +Causative]

a) Unlabelled tree

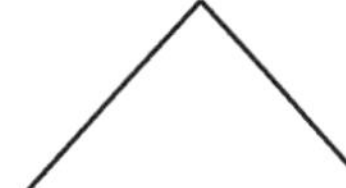

b) Morphemes and features insertion

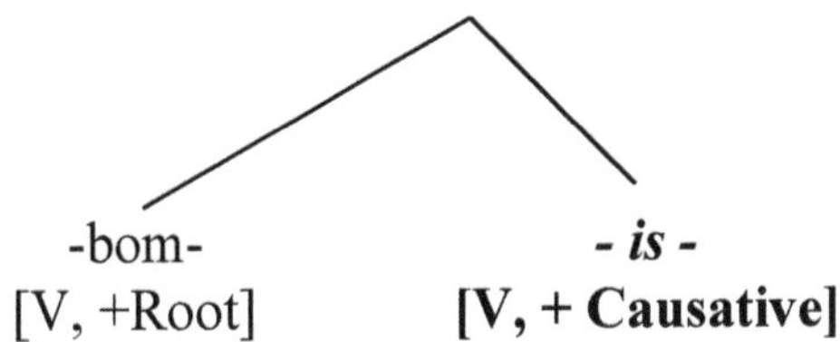

c)FPC I

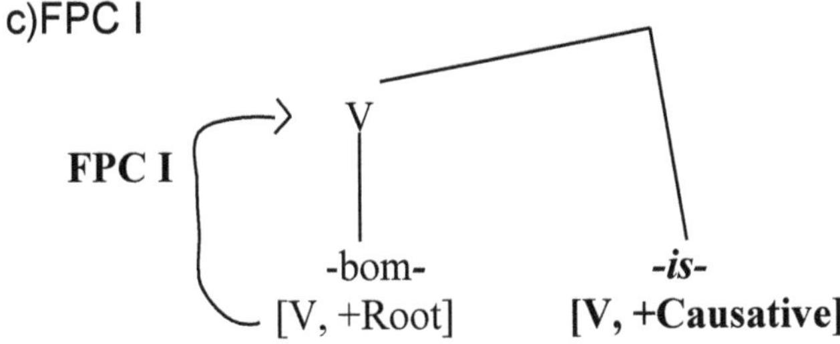

d) FPC II

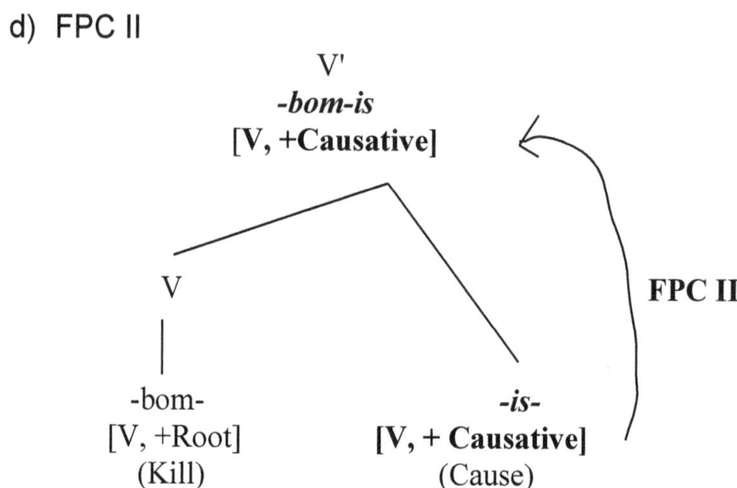

2.10. Summary

Lingala verb unit comprises a pre-stem made of a personal pronoun, a subject marker and the future prefix; a stem that contains the verb root and extension morphemes; and a post-stem which involves the perfect, habitual, present, past and infinitive markers. Clitics such as noun classes play a grammatical function in relative clauses, clefting and fronting. Lieber's morphological subcategorisation frames and feature percolation conventions theories have been used to examine Lingala verb structure in the framework of transformational generative grammar.

CHAPTER III: VALENCE CHANGING

Introduction

"Most languages have some verbal derivation that affects predicate arguments. Typically, they may reduce or increase the number of core arguments; alternatively, the number of core arguments may be retained but their semantic roles altered" (Dixon & Aikhenhvald, 2000:9).

Valence explores the way the relationship between arguments is affected. Valence alteration can be lexical, morphological and syntactic. Being a highly agglutinative language, Lingala valence changing is morphological. After exploring valence-decreasing and valence-increasing constructions, Marantz's (1984) 'merger' and Baker's 'incorporation' theories will be applied to Lingala data.

Finally, as a contribution, I will develop my theory called 'N-Tier Structure'.

3.1- Valence-decreasing

This includes the stative/resultative and the passive proper.

3.1.1- The stative/resultative

Consider the following rules:

(3.1)

a. NP1 V NP2

b. NP2 V'

Where V' represents the extended verb. These rules are exemplified as follows:

(3.2)

a. NP1 V NP2

mwana a – pas – ***ol*** -i molangi

Child 3SM-break-Rev-TS bottle

(The child has broken the bottle)

b. NP2 V'
mo-langi mo – pas – ***ok*** -i
3- bottle 3-break-***RESL***-TS

In (3.2)b. we explicitly ignore an agent is involved by just changing the reversive ***-ol-*** into stative/resultative -***ok.***

3.1.2- Proper Passive

The most telling valence-decreasing operation is passive. Lingala passive is synthetic (not analytic like in English). It does not require any kind of auxiliary but suffixing the passive morpheme ***-am-*** to the verb root. I distinguish between intransitive, transitive and impersonal passive.

3.1.2.1- Intransitive passive

This a case of a transitive verb to become intransitive, as in rules (3.3)

a. NP1 V NP2
b. NP2 V' (NP1)

(3.4)
a. NP1 V NP2
Yoane a – somb -i mbwa
John 3SM- buy- TS dog
(John has bought a dog)

b. NP2 V' (NP1)
mbwa e – somb – ***am*** -i (na Yoane)
dog 3SM-buy-***PASS***-TS (by John)
(The dog is bought (by John))

The active agent NP1 is "demoted" and becomes an oblique noun phrase (like the "by" phrase in English), while the subject NP2 is "promoted" to become agent.

3.1.2.2- Transitive passive

This is a case of a ditransitive verb to become (mono)-transitive, as in the rules below:

(3.5)
a. NP1 V NP2 NP3
b. NP3 V' NP2 (NP1)
c. NP2 V' NP3 (NP1)

(3.6)
a. NP1 V NP2 NP3
sango a – tey -i bandimi liloba
Priest 3SM-preach-T believers scriptures
(The priest has preached the scriptures to believers)

b. NP3 V' NP2 (NP1)
li-loba li – tey – ***am*** -i na bandimi (na sango)
5-scriptures 5-preach-***PASS***-TS to believers (by priest)
(The scripture is preached to the believers (by the priest)

c. NP2 V' NP3 (NP1)
bandimi ba – tey – ***am*** -i liloba (na sango)
2- Believers 2-preach-***PASS***-TS scripture (by priest)
(Believers have been preached the scriptures (by the priest))

In (3.6)b the indirect object NP3 is "promoted" to subject-hood, while the direct object NP2 functions as subject in (3.6)c. The "logical" subject NP1 becomes optional in both (3.6)b and (3.6)c.

3.1.2.3- Impersonal Passive

Intransitive verbs can also be "passivised", with the result that the subject is omitted, as in the following example:

(3.7)

a. NP1 V

b. ф V'

(3.8)

a. NP1 V

mwana a – sok – ***ol*** -i

Child SM-wash-stative-TS

(The child has washed)

b. ф V'

a – sok – ***w*** – ***am*** – i

3SM-wash-***PASS***-TS

(He has been washed)

As the subject NP1 is reflected in the verb unit by the subject marker (SM), it can be omitted when the verb is turned into passive. I call it "Zero Passive."

3.1.3. The Proto Bantu Passive

The sentence (3.8)b is a case of double passive. It is a combination of the Proto Bantu passive ***-w-*** and the proper passive ***-am-***, commonly used in Lingala. This occurs when some verbs extended with **-ol-** are passivized, as exemplified below:

(3.9)

ko-sak-***ol***-a	"to disclose"
ko-sak-***w-am***-a	"to be disclosed"
ko-pamb-***ol***-a	"to bless"
ko-pamb-***w-am***-a	"to be blessed"
ko-bong-***ol***-a	"to change"
ko-bong-***w-am***-a	"to be transformed"

ko-bak-***ol***-a “to cut (tree)
ko-bak-***w-am***-a “to be cut”

ko-tong-***ol***-a ”to inject anally”
ko-tong-***w-am***-a “to be injected anally”

ko-fong-ol-a “to open”
ko-fong-***w-am-a*** “to be opened”

Apart from its syntactic role in (3.9), the passive ***-w-*** plays a semantic role also by altering the meaning of the verb:

(3.10)
ko-kang-a “to tie”
ko-kang-***ol***-a “to untie”
ko-kang-***am***-a “to be tied/caught/arrested”
ko-kang-***w-am***-a “to be delivered from a curse”

ko-bot-a “to give birth”
ko-bot-***am***-a “to be born”
ko-bot-***w-am***-a “to be born again (be baptised)”

ko-kab-a “to give”
ko-kab-***ol***-a “to divide/share”
ko-kab-***w-an***-a “to be separated from each other”

3.1.3.1. Passivised verb root

After deeply analysing some verbs in Lingala, I have come to the conclusion that the proto-Bantu passive ***-w-*** does not occur in some cases as an independent entity. It is part of what I call “passivized” verb roots, which have a passive meaning in themselves. Examples are exemplified in (3.11):

(3.11)
ko-lang***w***-a 'to be drunk'
ko-sek***w***-a 'to be resuscitated'
ko-kam***w***-a 'to be astonished'
ko-samb***w***-a 'to be vilipended'

(3.12)
Ba-to ba-lang***w***-i
2-person 2SM-drink-***Pass***-TS
(People are drunk)

(3.13)
Ba-weyi ba-ko-sek***w***-a na mokolo ya suka
2-dead 2-SM-FUT-resuscitate-***Pass***-FV in day of last
(The dead are to resuscitate in the last day)

3.1.4 - The Reflexive

With morphological reflexive, the reduction in semantic valence is reflected in a corresponding reduction in grammatical valence (Payne, 2006).

The reflexive affix ***-mi-*** reduces a transitive verb into intransitive. Below are rules and examples:
(3.14)

a. NP1 V NP2
b. NP2 V'
c. ф V'

(3.15)

a. NP1 V NP2
mama a-sok-ol-i mwana
Mum SM-wash-TS child
(Mum has washed the child)

b. NP2 V'
mwana a – ***mi*** – sok- ol -i
Child SM- ***Refl***-wash-TS
(The child has washed himself)

c. ф V'
a – ***mi*** – sok-ol -i
SM- ***Refl***-wash-TS
(He has washed himself)

The SM is co-referential to the logical object NP2, which is "promoted" as subject in (3.15)b. In this case the subject can be omitted as he is doing the action to himself, reflected in the subject marker as in (3.15)c.

3.2 – Valence-increasing

Valence increasing includes causative and the applied verb construction.

3.2.1. Causative

Lingala has a morphological causative, a device for creating verbs which means "to cause X verb to verb" from a form "X verb". There are two types of causative: the causative from intransitive verbs and the one from transitive verbs.

3.2.1.1 Causative from intransitive verbs

Illustrations are provided in rules (3.16) and sentences (3.17) below:
(3.16)
a. NP1 V
b. NP0 V' NP1

(3.17)

a. NP1 V
Yoane a – lel -i
John 3SM-cry-TS
(John has cried)

b. NP0 V' NP1
mama a – lel – ***is*** -i Yoane
Mum 3SM-cry-***Caus***-TS Jonh
(Mum has made John cry)

The "logical" subject NP1 becomes an object and there is an introduction of a new syntactic subject NP0.

3.2.1.2- Causative from transitive verbs

The causative from transitive verbs is exemplified as follows:

(3.18)

a. NP1 V NP2
b. NP0 V' NP1 NP2

(3.19)

a. NP1 V NP2
Petelo a – tang -i buku
Peter SM-read-TS book
(Peter has read the book)

b. NP0 V' NP1 NP2
molakisi a–tang – ***is*** -i Petelo buku
Teacher SM-read-***Caus***-TS Peter book
(The teacher has made Peter read the book)

From the English glossary "make" constitutes what is called an Exceptional Case Marking (ECM) verb. It is a hallmark of syntactic approaches that the causative affix be regarded as an ECM verb (Spencer, 1991).

3.2.2. Applicative/benefactive

The applicative extension “applies” the action of the verb to an expressed object and is usually translated by the English preposition “to” or “for”. For this reason, it is also called “the prepositional” extension.

Consider the rules (3.20):
(3.20)

a. NP1 V NP2
b. NP1 V' NP3 NP2

An example is given as follows:

(3.21)
a. NP1 V NP2
Malia a -lamb- i soso
Mary SM-cook-TS chicken
(Mary has cooked chicken)

b. NP1 V' NP3 NP2
Malia a- lamb- ***el*** -i bana soso
Mary SM-cook-***Appl***-TS children chicken
(Mary has cooked chicken for children)

3.3. Marantz's (1984) “Merger” Theory

Marantz's 'merger' theory shows how the causative, applicative and passive morphemes, which at first act as independent entities, 'merge' with the verb unit in a tree structure. He used data from Chi-mwini, a highly morphological Bantu language, to illustrate his theory.

3.3.1. Causative merger

What is interesting is that Chi-mwini and Lingala morphological passive are closely similar, as shown in the following data:

(3.22) Chi-mwini (Marantz, 1984)

a.

NP1	V	NP2
wa:na	wa-andik-ize	Xati
child	subj-write-T/A	letter

(The child wrote letter)

b.

NP0	V'	NP1	NP2
mwalimu	wa-andik-***ish***-ize	wa:na	Xati
teacher	subj-write-***Caus***-T/A	child	letter

(The teacher made the children write a letter)

(3.23) Lingala

a.

NP1	V	NP2
mwana	a- kom -i	mokanda
child	SM-read-TS	letter

(The child has written a letter)

b.

NP0	V'	NP1	NP2
molakisi	a–kom – ***is***-i	mwana	mokanda
teacher	SM-write-***Caus***-TS	child	letter

(The teacher has made the child write a letter)

To illustrate his "merger" theory, Marantz provides a lexical structure, a logico-semantic (l-s) structure and a S structure representations.

3.3.1.1. Lexical structure

At this level, roots and affixes are provided together with their lexical entries containing information about transitivity and semantic roles assigned to.

Illustration is provided in (3.24): Chi-mwini/Lingala

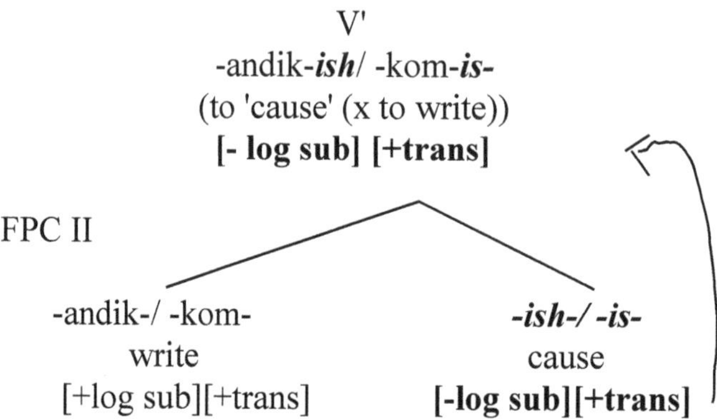

Following is the lexical entry of the causative affix ***-ish-/-is-***:

(3.25)

-***ish-/-is-***] V ------- , [-log sub][+transitive]

What is noticed is that the input sentences (3.22)a and (3.23)a have logical subjects NP1. In the output sentences (3.22)b and (3.23)b, the causative verb admits a new syntactic subject NP0 , and the logical subject NP1 becomes an object.

I have applied Lieber's FPC II (cf.chap 2.9.2) to show that the causative affix functions as the HEAD of the extended verb, its features [-log][+transitive] are passed up to the causative verb.

3.3.1.2. Logico-semantic (l-s) structure

At the l-s structure, the causative affix is independent from the verb unit. It has its own node, as shown in the tree diagram (3.26):

(3.26) I-s structure

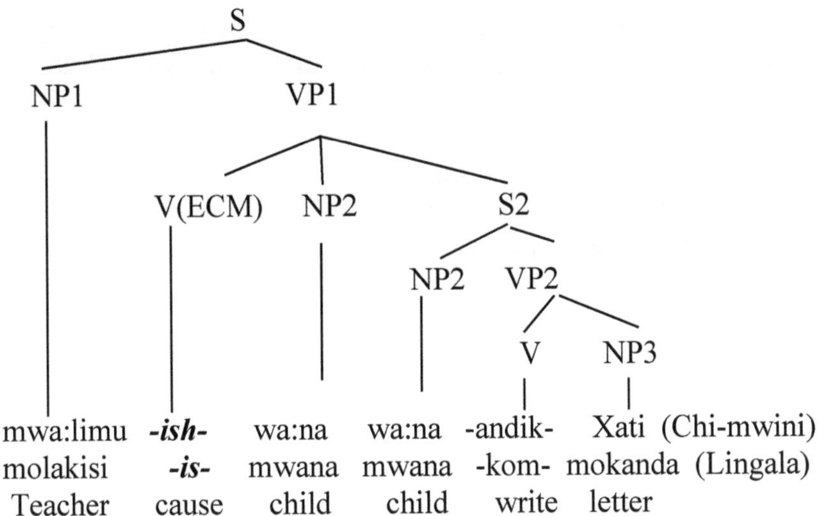

At the I-s structure, the causative affix functions as the Exceptional Case Marking (ECM) verb "cause" in English.

3.3.1.3. S structure

At the S structure below, the affix (V1) and the root (V2) "merge" into the causative verb V'.

(3.27)

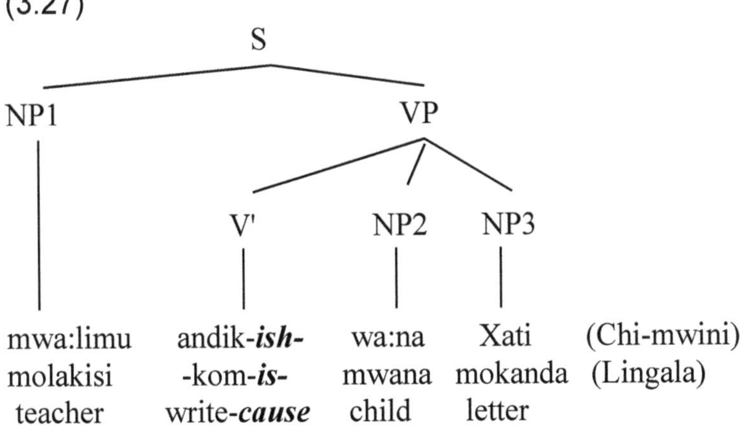

3.3.2. Passive merger

Modelling on Marantz's approach, I am going to analyse Lingala passive merger. Let us consider the following data:

(3.28)

a. NP1 V NP2
Petelo a-tong-i ndako
Peter SM-build-TS house
(Peter has built a house)

b. NP2 V' (NP1)
ndako e-tong-***am*** -i (na Petelo)
house SM-build-***PASS***-TS (by Peter)
(The house is built by Peter)

In the passive sentence (3.28)b, the object NP2 is "promoted" to subject-hood and the logical subject NP1 is "demoted" to become an optional object.

3.3.2.1. Lexical structure

The lexical entry of the passive morpheme ***-am-*** is:

(3.29)

-am-] V------ , [-log sub][-transitive]

The lexical structure of the passive will be:

(3.30)

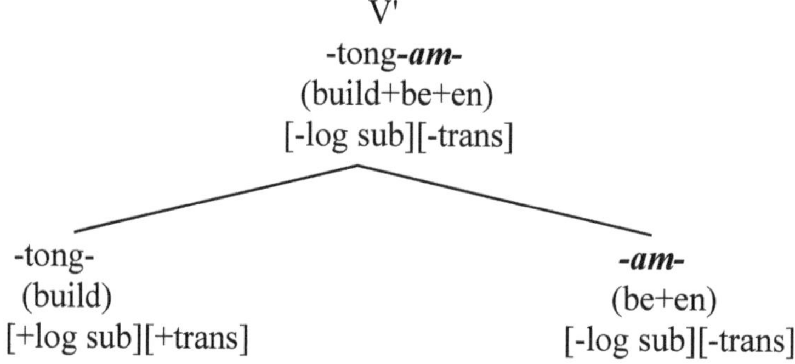

3.3.2.2. Logico-semantic structure

Below are the l-s structure and S structure of the passive sentence (3.31)b:

(3.31)

S1

NP1 VP1

V(Aux) S2

NP1 VP2

V NP2

Petelo	*-am-*	Petelo	-tong-	ndako
Peter	be+en	Peter	build	house
(Peter has been)		(Peter builds a house)		

At the l-s structure, the passive affix act ***-am-*** as the passive verb "be+en" in English, with its own V node.

3.3.2.3. S structure

(3.32)

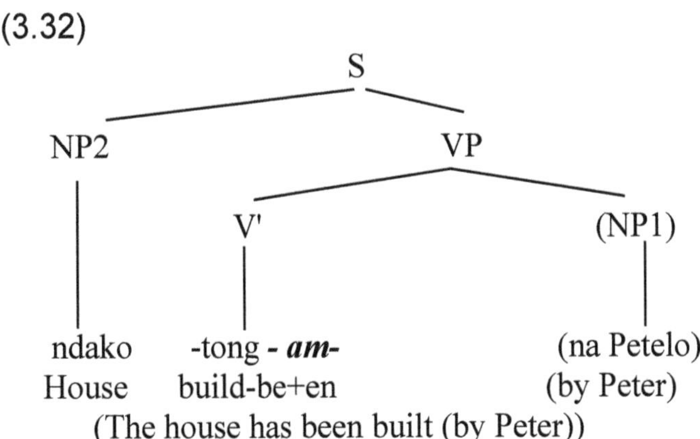

It is at the S structure (3.32) that the passive morpheme ceases to behave like an independent verb and “merges” with the verb unit.

3.3.3. Applicative merger

Let us consider the applied sentence in (3.33)b :
(3.33)

a. NP1 V NP2
Petelo a-tong-i ndako
Peter SM-build-TS house
(Peter has built a house)

b. NP1 V' NP3 NP2
Petelo a-tong-***el***-i Malako ndako
Peter SM-build-***APPL***-TS Marcus house
(Peter has built a house for Marcus)

3.3.3.1. Lexical structure

The lexical entry of the applicative is:
(3.34) ***-el-***] V-------, 'for' (benefactive), [+transitive]

The lexical structure of the applied verb is provided as follows:

(3.35)

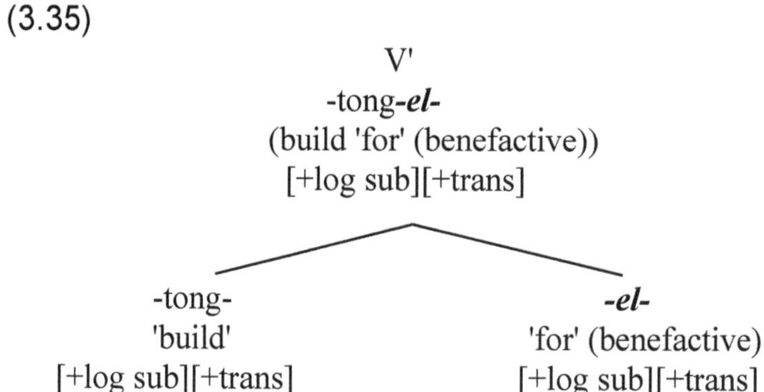

3.3.3.2. Logico-semantic (l-s) structure

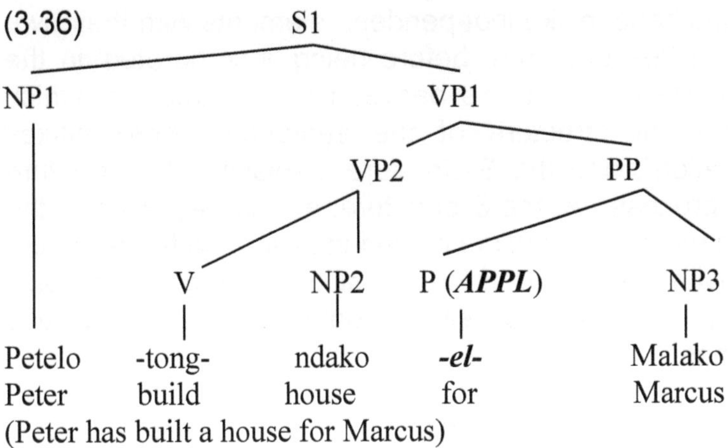

In the structure (3.36), the applicative ***-el-*** functions as an underlying preposition.

3.3.3.3. S structure

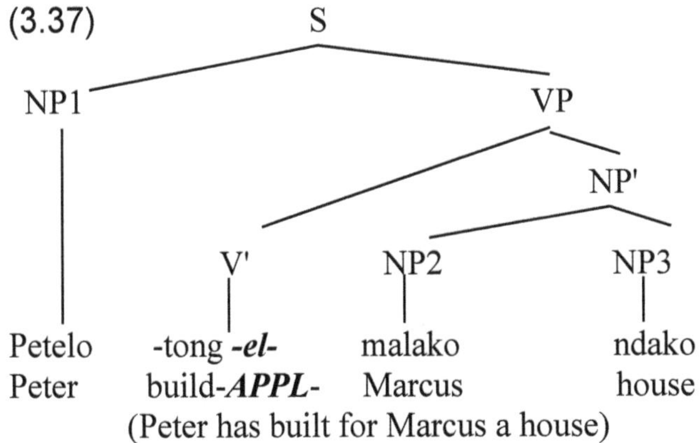

At the S structure, the applied morpheme 'merges' with the verb root to form an applied verb construction.

3.4. Baker's "incorporation" theory (1988)

Baker has developed the 'incorporation' theory to explain the way affixes behave like independent elements with their own nodes in a tree structure, before being 'incorporated' in the verb unit. He distinguishes between the D-structure, which represents the structure of the sentence before affixes "incorporation", and the S-structure displaying the structure after the process. At the S-structure, a trace *(*$\mathbf{e}_i$*)* is left in the environment that the affix occupied initially. The trace *(*$\mathbf{e}_i$*)* co-indexes with the affix in its new position. I am going to apply the 'incorporation' theory using Lingala Future and Reflexive morphemes.

3.4.1. Future 'incorporation'

Given the future sentence in (3.38):

(3.38)

Petelo	a-***ko***-tong-a	ndaku
Peter	SM-***FUT***-build-FV	house

(Peter will build a house)

3.4.1.1. D-structure

The D-structure of (3.38) is shown below, where the future morpheme functions as the auxiliary 'will' in English.

(3.39)

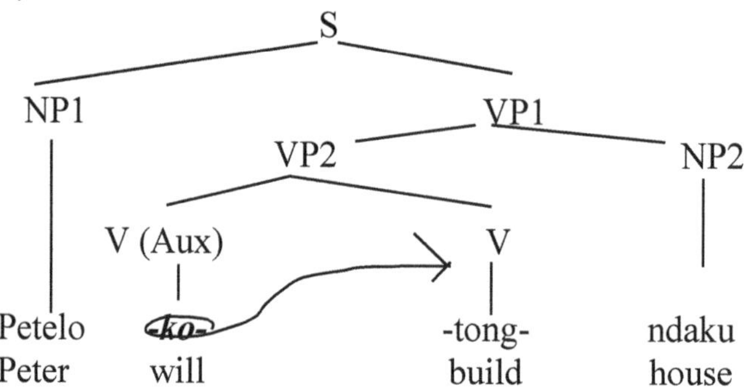

At the D-structure the future affix has its own V node. It is 'incorporated' in the main verb to form one morphological unit at the S-structure (3.40) below:

3.4.1.2- S-structure

(3.40)

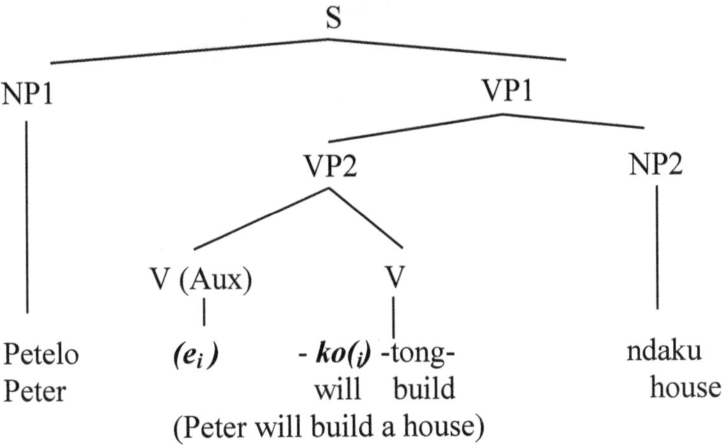

The future morpheme -***ko***- 'incorporates' into the verb root, but leaves a trace ***(e****i****)*** in its previous position.

3.4.2. The reflexive 'incorporation'

Let us consider the reflexive sentence in (3.41):

(3.41)
Malako a- ***mi***-buk-i lokolo
Marcus SM-***REFL***-break-ts leg
(Marcus has broken the leg himself)

3.4.2.1- D-structure

(3.42)

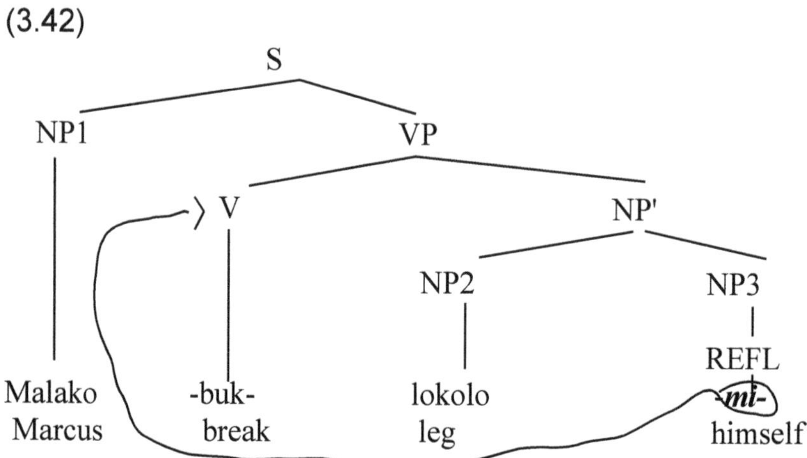

The reflexive affix ***-mi-*** acts as the independent reflexive pronoun 'oneself'. The arrow shows 'Incorporation' movement.

3.4.2.2- S-structure

The S-structure of the sentence (3.41) is:
(3.43)

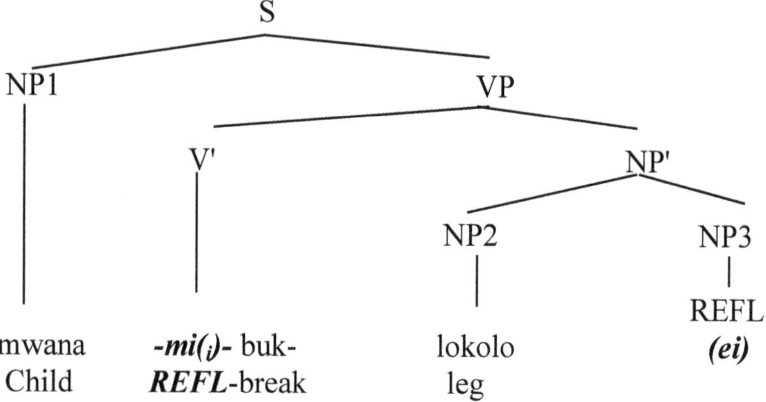

The reflexive affix is 'incorporated' in the verb unit, but leaves a trace ***(ei)*** in its previous environment, which co-indexes with the affix in its new position.

3.5. Summary

Extensions are very important morphological particles in Bantu grammar in that they alter the argument of the verb. The passive and stative extensions reduce the valence of the verb, while the causative and applicative increase it. Marantz 'merger' and Baker's 'incorporation' theories have similarities as they represent sentences at surface and deep structures. I do prefer to stand by Marantz due to the fact that he provides an independent structure of the extended outside the sentence.

CHAPTER IV: N-TIER STRUCTURE THEORY:

Introduction

Marantz' and Baker's theories are a worthy contribution to the phenomenon of morphological valence changing. Both theories were previously applied in my MA dissertation (R. Batota-Mpeho. 2002). As a complementary contribution, I have developed a theory called **N-Tier Structure (NTS)** in which syntactic, semantic, morphological, lexical and phonological information are displayed on different tiers or layers in the same structure.

4.1. N-Tier Structure (NTS) Theory

This theory is modelled on N-Tier Architecture used in software engineering. It refers to the architecture of an application that has at least 3 "logical" layers that are separate. Each layer interacts with only the one directly below, and has a specific function that it is responsible for. In the term "N-Tier", "N" implies any number of distinct tiers used in architecture (or structure).

In my theory, tree structures are composed of at least three or all of the following tiers:

- **Syntactic Tier,** which provides syntactic functions of each part of the sentence.
- **Semantic Tier,** which gives information on semantic roles assigned to each component of the sentence.
- **Morphological Tier**, which contains information on different morphemes that form verb units and noun phrases.
- **Lexical tier,** which displays lexical components of the sentence with their distinct morphemes.
- **Phonological Tier,** which explains phonological rules taking place in affixation. This tier is optional and less applied.

I distinguish between input NTS, which displays tree structures before the change of valence, and output NTS after the valence has been altered.

4.1.1. Passive Structure

Let us consider the following sentences:

(4.1) Input sentence

NP1 V NP2
Sofele a- sal -i likama
car SM-make-TS accident
(The driver has made an accident)

(4.2) Output sentence

NP2 V' (NP1)
li-kama li- ***sal -am*** -i (na sofele)
Accident SM-make-PASS-TS (by driver)
(The accident is made (by the drive)

The NTS of the passive verb base ***-sal-am-*** is as follow:

(4.3)

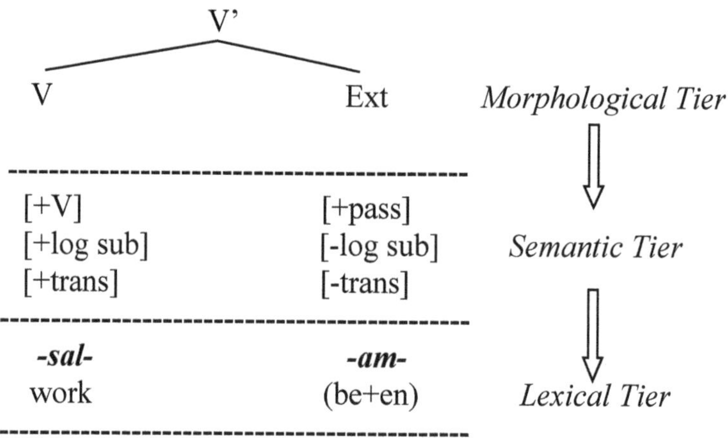

The features of the passive affix ***-am-*** ([+pass], [-log sub] and [-trans] constitute the head of the sentence (4.2).

Below are the NTS of the sentences (4.1) and (4.2):

(4.4) Input NTS:

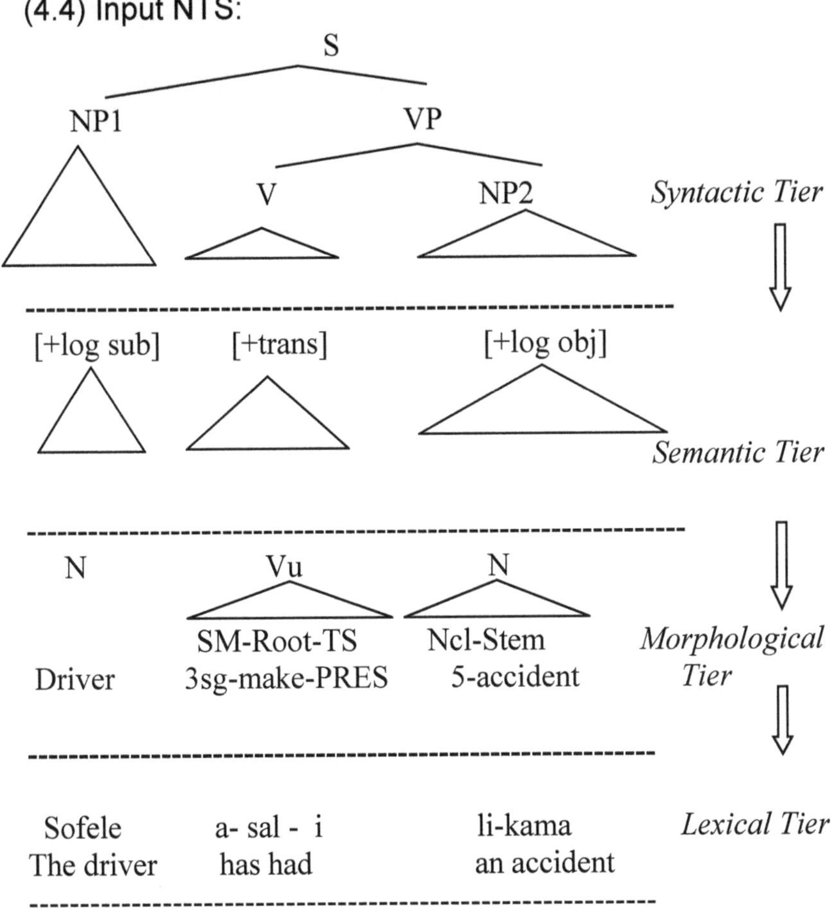

Interpretation: This is a typical SVO sentence, with a transitive verb [+trans]. NP1 is the logical subject [+log sub] and NP2 the logical object [+log obj].

(4.5) Output NTS:

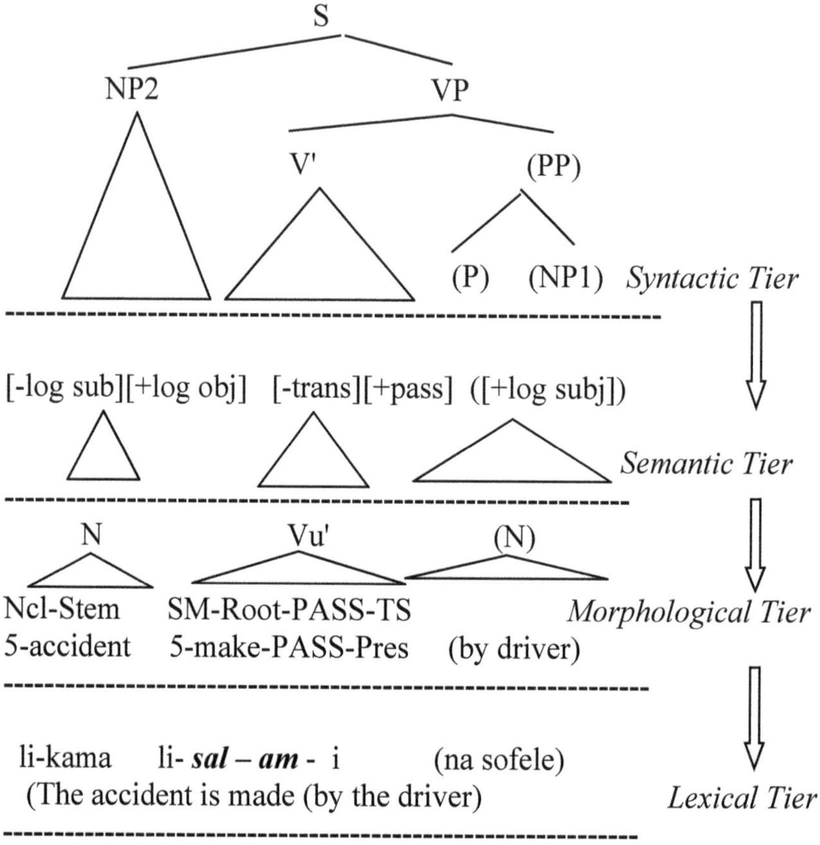

S

NP2 VP

V' (PP)

(P) (NP1) *Syntactic Tier*

[-log sub][+log obj] [-trans][+pass] ([+log subj])

Semantic Tier

N Vu' (N)

Ncl-Stem SM-Root-PASS-TS *Morphological Tier*

5-accident 5-make-PASS-Pres (by driver)

----

li-kama li- ***sal*** – ***am*** - i (na sofele)

(The accident is made (by the driver) *Lexical Tier*

Interpretation: NP2 is 'promoted' as syntactic subject [-log sub], while NP1 becomes an optional object. The passive affix has turned the verb into intransitive [-trans].

The subject noun class prefix ***li-*** is in agreement with the subject maker.

4.1.2. Causative Structure

Below is exemplified a causative sentence transformation:

(4.6) Input sentence
NP1 V
lolemo lo-zik -i
Tongue SM-burn-TS
(The tongue has burnt)

(4.7) Output sentence
NP0 V' NP1
mwana a-zik – is -i lolemo
Child SM-burn-CAUS-TS tongue
(The child has the tongue burnt)

Below is the NTS of the causative verb ***–zik-is-*** (cause to burn):

(4.8)

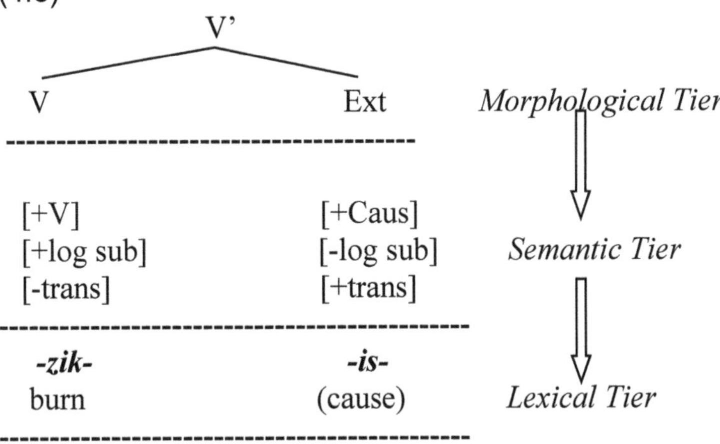

The causative affix ***-is-***, which is the head, has conveyed its semantic features to the sentence (4.7).

The NTS of sentences (4.6) and (4.7) are as follows:

(4.9) Input NTS:

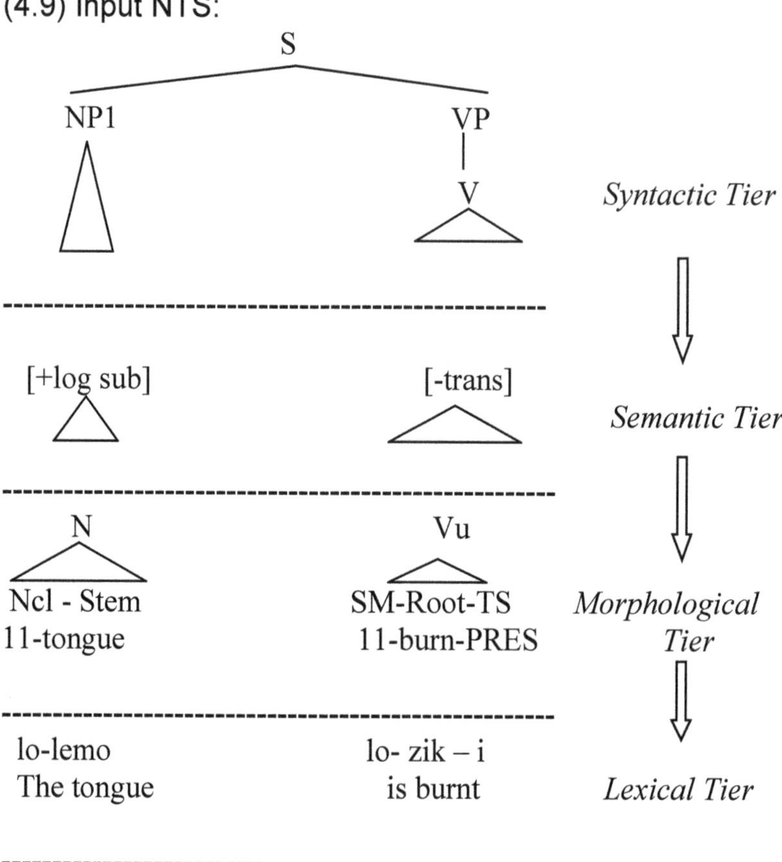

Interpretation: NP1 functions as the logical subject [+log sub], while its noun class prefix ***lo-*** is co-indexed to the intransitive [-trans] verb unit as subject marker (SM).

(4.10) Output NTS:

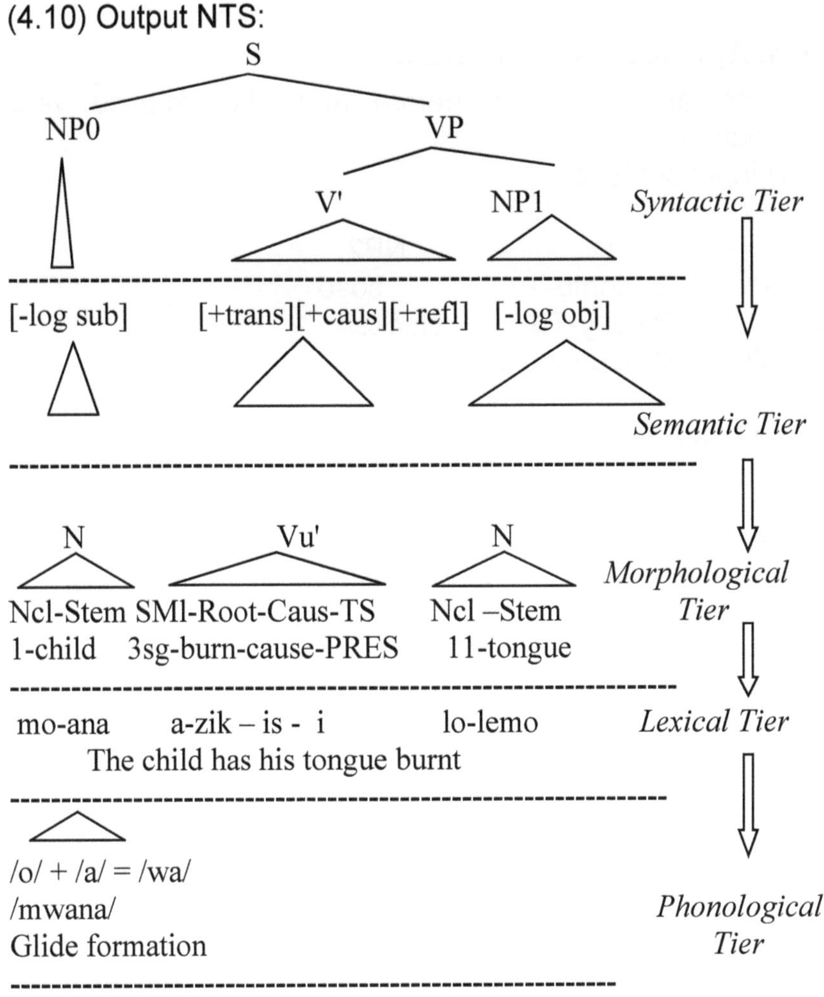

Interpretation: After the causative process, a new syntactic subject NP0 [-log sub] is introduced and the logical subject NP1 is 'demoted' as syntactic object [-log obj]. The verb becomes transitive [+trans] and reflexive [+Refl] as NP0 is doing action to himself. The 3sg pronoun ***a-*** (co-referring to the subject NP0) is used as subject marker. Phonologically, the noun *mo-ana* is realised as /mwana/ after glide formation has taken place.

4.1.3. Applicative Structure

Following are sentences before and after applied verb construction:

(4.11) Input sentence

NP1	V	NP2
mama	a- somb- i	soso
Mum	SM-buy-TS	chicken

(Mum has bought chicken)

(4.12) Output sentence

NP1	V'	NP3	NP2
mama	a – somb- el-i	bana	soso
mum	SM-buy-APPL-TS	children	chicken

(Mum has bought chicken for children)

The NTS of the applied verb ***-somb-el-*** ('to buy for') is:

(4.13)

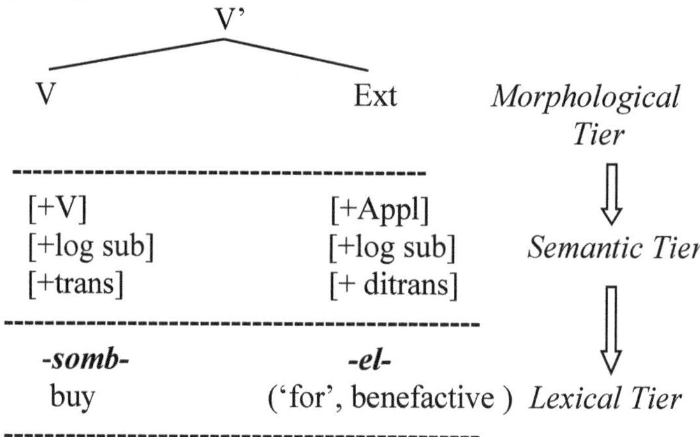

The extension ***-el-*** is the head of the sentence (4.13) in that it transfers its semantic features [+Appl] [+log sub] [+ditrans] to the whole sentence.

N-Tier tree structures of sentences (4.11) and (4.12) are given below:

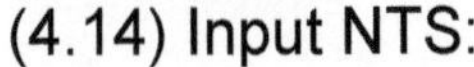

(4.14) Input NTS:

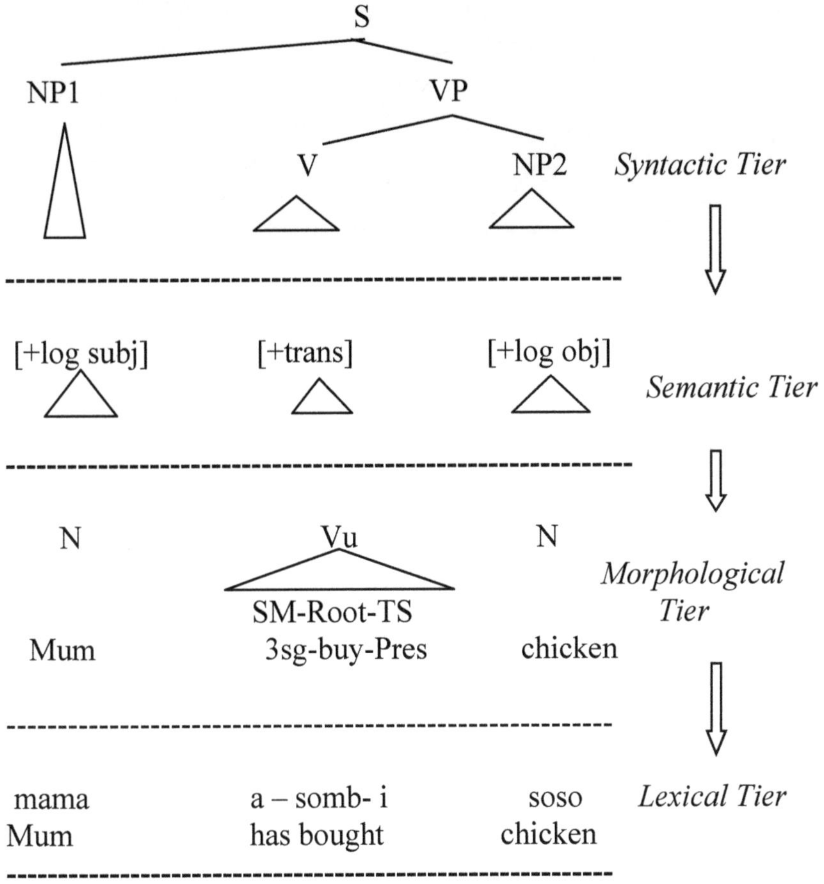

S

NP1 VP

V NP2 *Syntactic Tier*

[+log subj] [+trans] [+log obj] *Semantic Tier*

N Vu N

SM-Root-TS

Morphological Tier

Mum 3sg-buy-Pres chicken

mama a – somb- i soso *Lexical Tier*

Mum has bought chicken

(4.15) Output NTS:

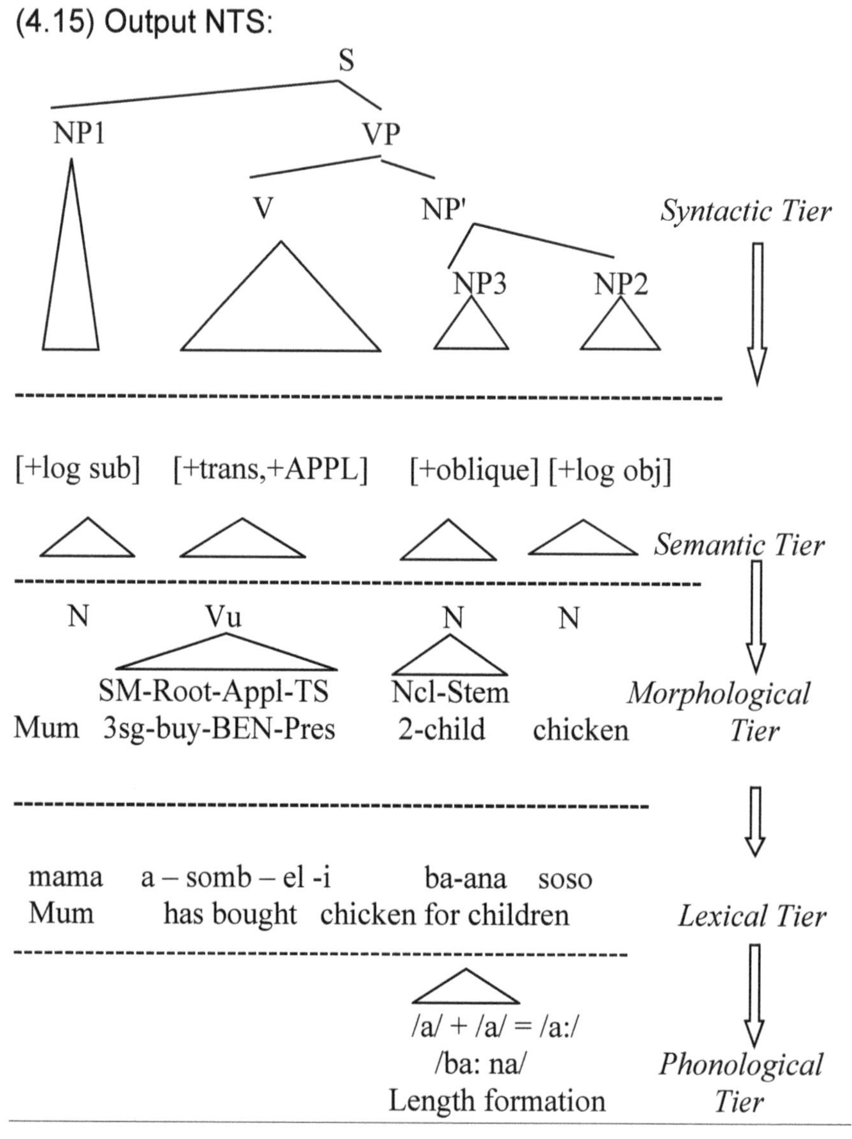

Interpretation: The applicative extension has transformed the transitive [+trans] verb into di-transitive [+ditrans], with the introduction of an oblique object [+oblique] NP3. Phonologically, the noun *ba-na* is realised as /ba:na/ after vowel length formation.

4.2. Application of NTS theory in English

4.2.1. English Passive

NTS theory is applicable to English sentence transformation such as passive. Let us first consider the input active sentence (4.16):

(4.16)
Children ate mangoes.

The simple past sentence (4.16) may be turned into passive with different tenses as follows:

(4.17) Simple past
Mangoes were eaten (by children)

(4.18) Past perfect
Mangoes had been eaten (by children)

(4.19) Future perfect
Mangoes will have been eaten (by children)

(4.20) Present perfect progressive
Mangoes were being eaten (by children)

(4.21) Past perfect progressive
Mangoes had been being eaten (by children)

(4.22) Future perfect progressive
Mangoes will be being eaten (by children)

4.2.2. Passive N-Tier Structures

The NTS of the input active sentence (4.16) is given in (4.23), while NTS of output sentences (4.17) - (4.22) are provided in (4.24) -(4.29) below.

(4.23) Input NTS: Children ***ate*** mangoes

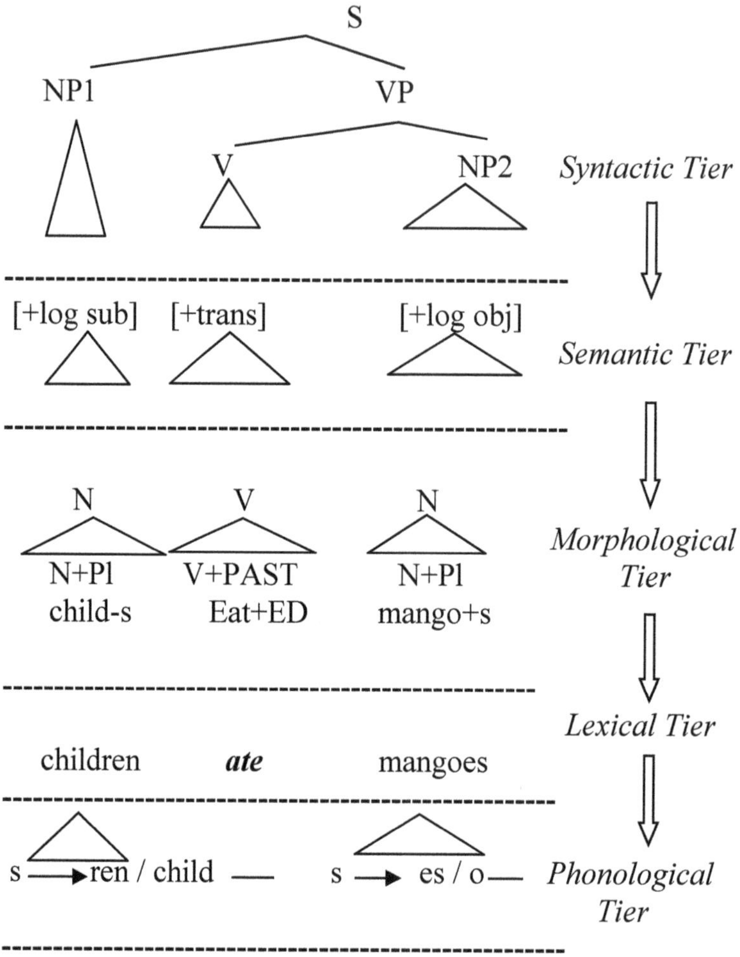

Morphologically, the irregular verb is marked with the past tense affix -ED. Two phonological rules apply. 1) The plural -*s* is realised as *-ren* after the noun *child.* 2) *-s* is realised as -es in the environment after some nouns ending with the phoneme /o/

(4.24) Output NTS: mangoes ***were eaten*** (by children)

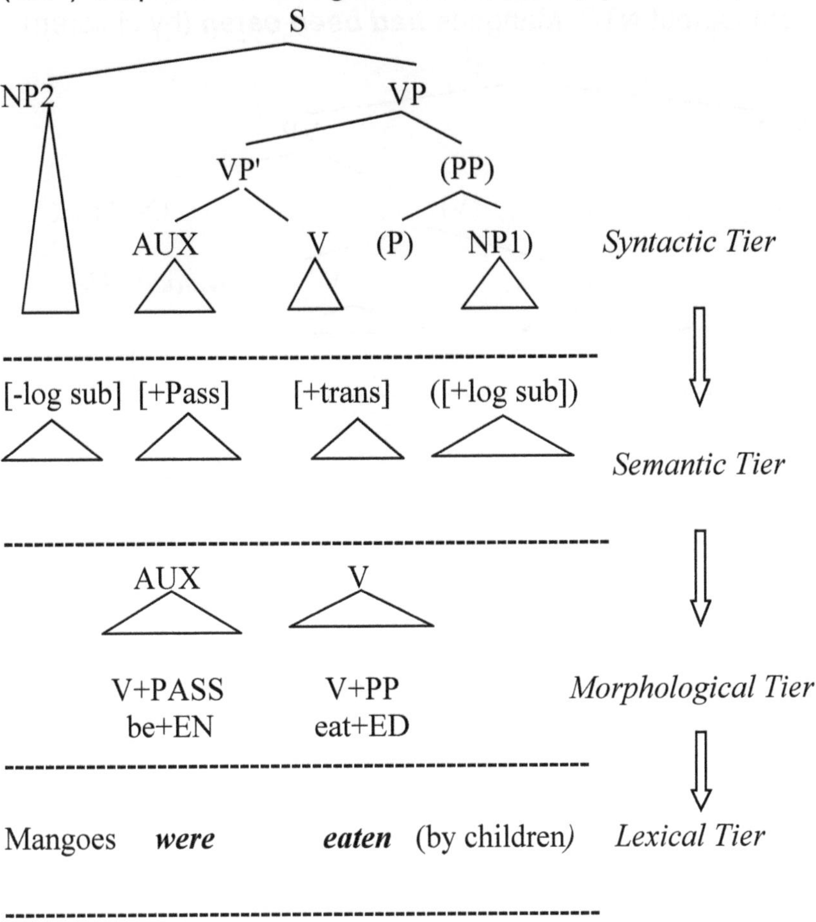

The passive is expressed by the affix –EN, while –ED is used to form the past participle even though it is irregular in EATEN. The logical subject becomes an optional object.

(4.25) Output NTS: Mangoes ***had been eaten*** (by children)

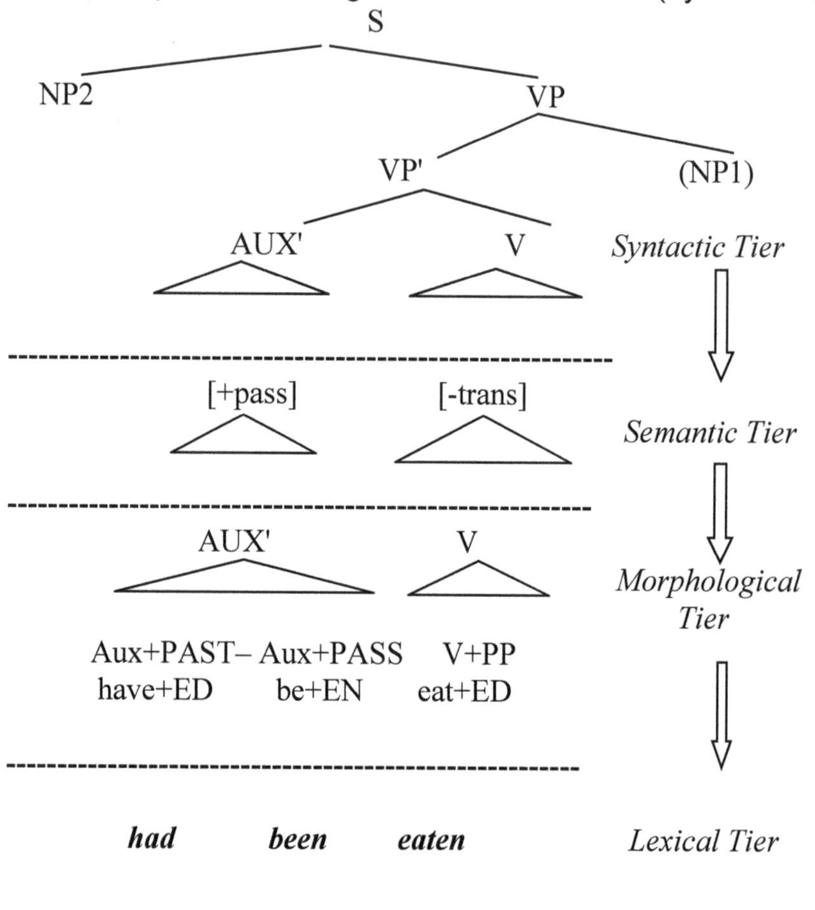

Morphologically, the verb phrase is made of the auxiliary BE in past perfect, followed by the past participle of the main verb EAT, which becomes intransitive by being "passivized".

(4.26) Output NTS: Mangoes ***will have been eaten*** (by children)

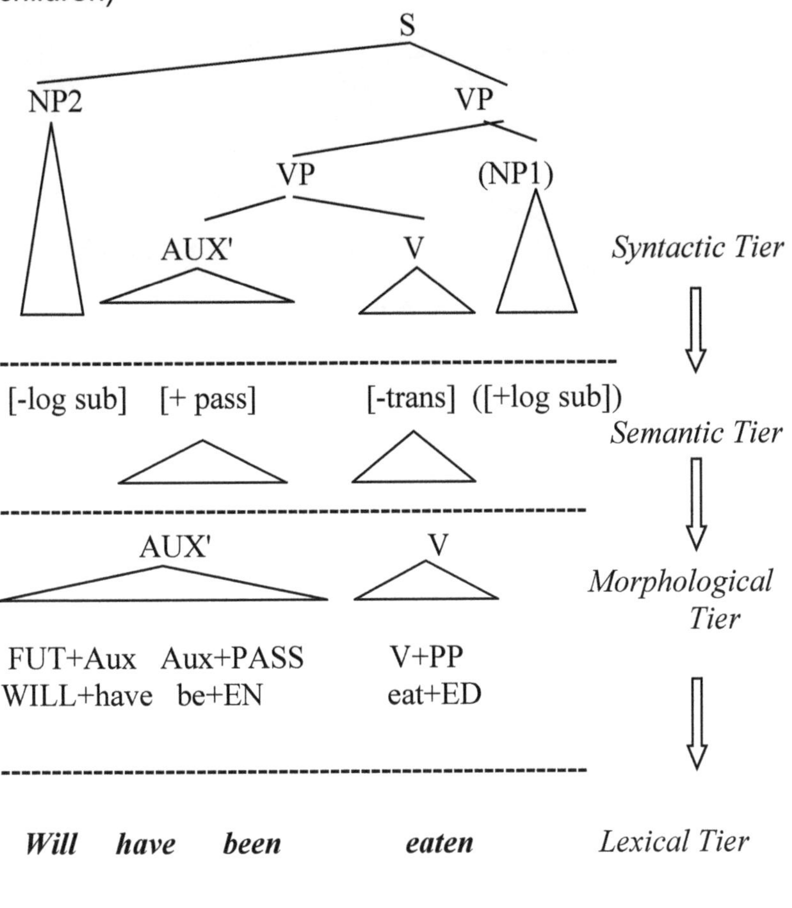

This complex construction is less used in the spoken language. The auxiliary AUX' is made of the verb *be* in future perfect.

(4.27) Output NTS: Mangoes ***were being eaten*** (by children)

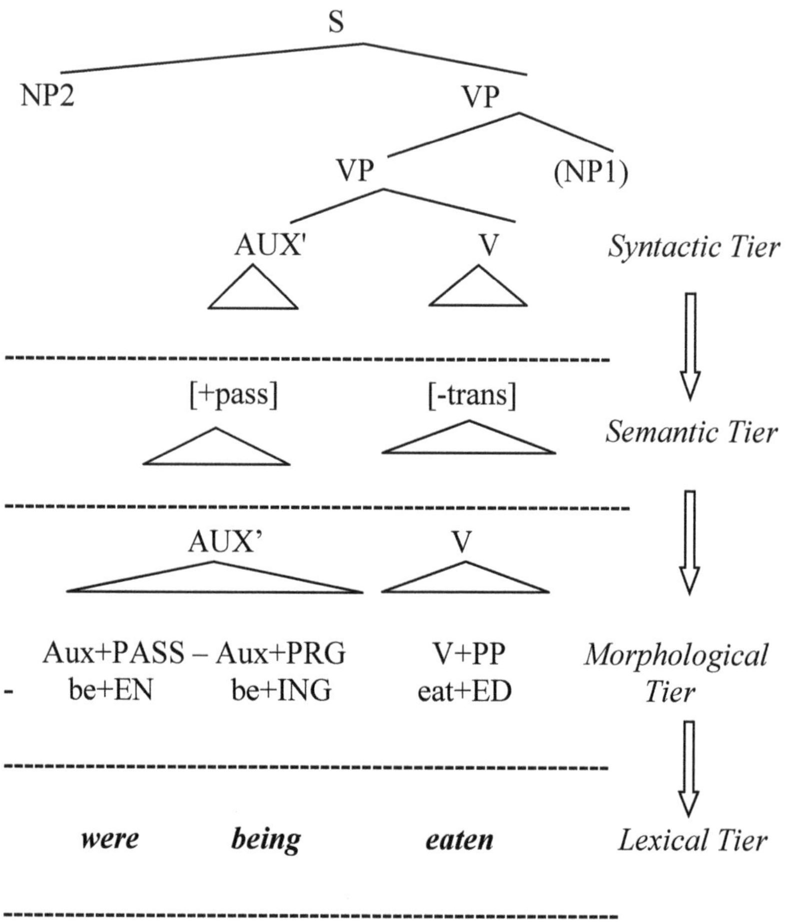

-ING is the progressive morpheme and always occur with the auxiliary *be.*

(4.28) Output NTS: Mangoes ***had been being eaten*** (by children)

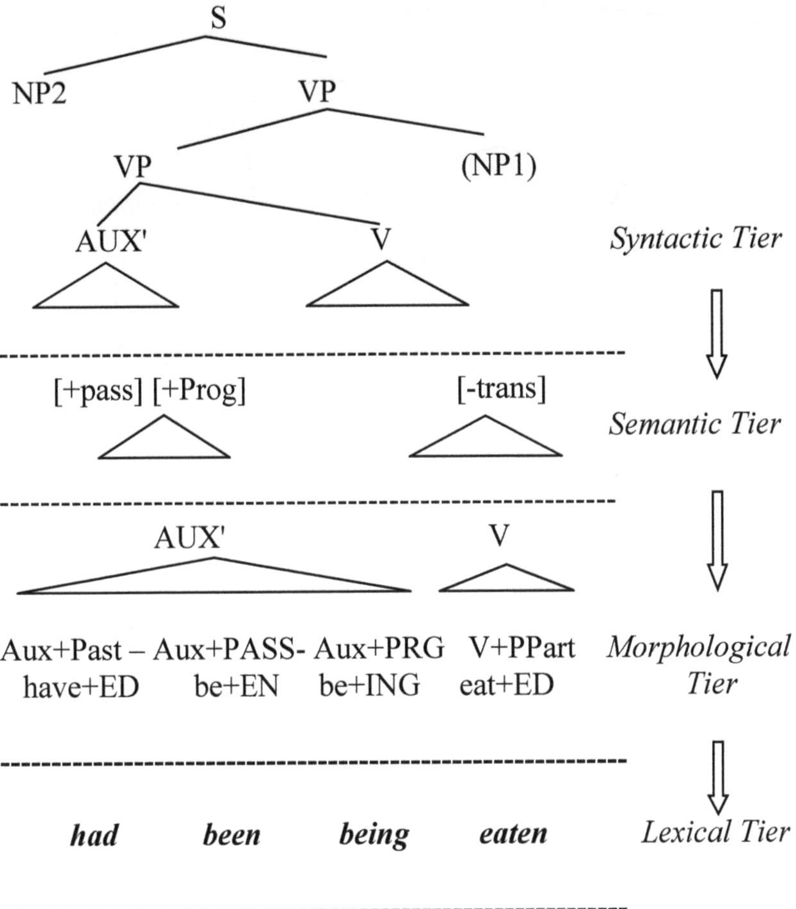

This is made of the auxiliary *be* in past perfect continuous.

(4.29) Output NTS: Mangoes ***will have been being eaten*** (by children)

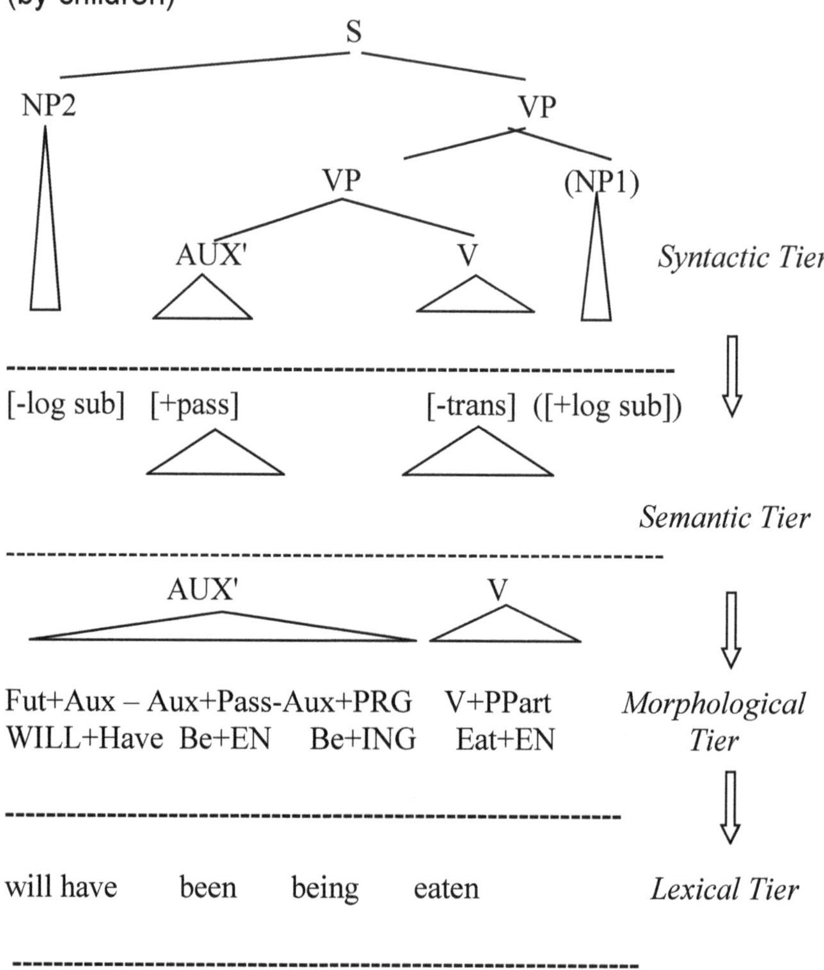

This is the most complex transformation as it is composed of five auxiliary. It needs a good grasp of grammar in order to be understood.

4.3. NTS and complex words

As a generative theory, NTS may be applied to word formation. Each morpheme, bound or free, is provided with a semantic feature showing to which morphological category it belongs. If they occur, phonological rules that apply in affixation are displayed. Following are illustrations in which English and Lingala complex words are examined in the framework of NTS.

4.3.1 English complex words

Examples are provided with the following words: *faithfulness* (4.30), *unfortunately* (4.31), *unplugged* (4.32) and *cut* (4.33).

(4.30) **faithfulness**

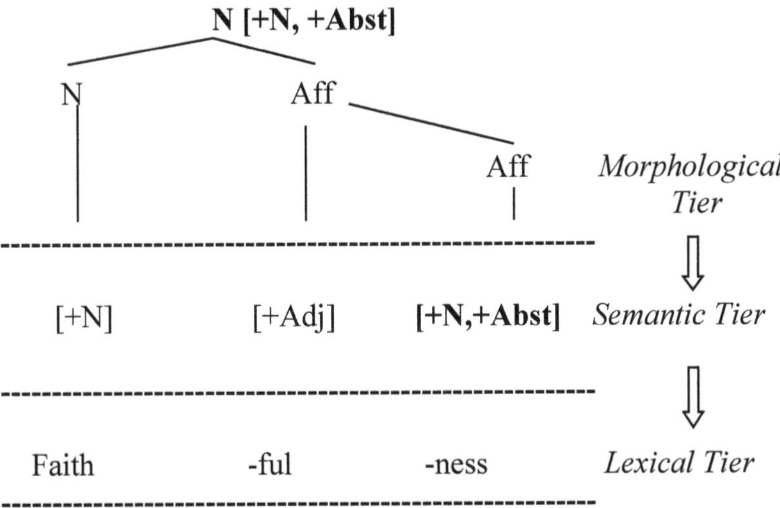

In this structure, *-ful* [+Adj] is affixed to the noun *faith* [+N] to form an adjective, while *–ness* [+N, +Abst] changes the adjective into an abstract noun and constitutes the Head of the noun, passing its features to the top node N.

(4.31) **unfortunately**

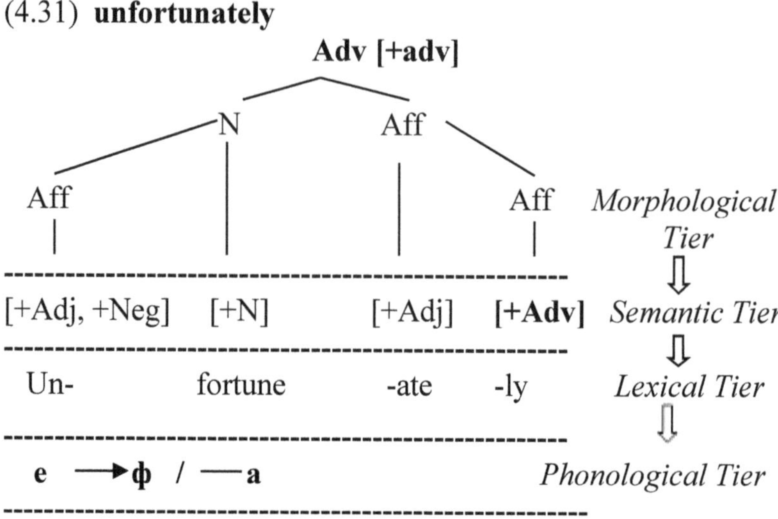

The prefix *un-* [+Adj, +Neg] is attached to adjective *fortunate* to give it a negative meaning, whereas *–ly* [+Adv] changes the adjective into an adverb, hence it is the Head of the word, 'percolating' its semantic features to the top node Adv The phonological rule says that the last vowel of *fortun(e)* is not realised when suffixed by *-ate*

(4.32) **unplugged**

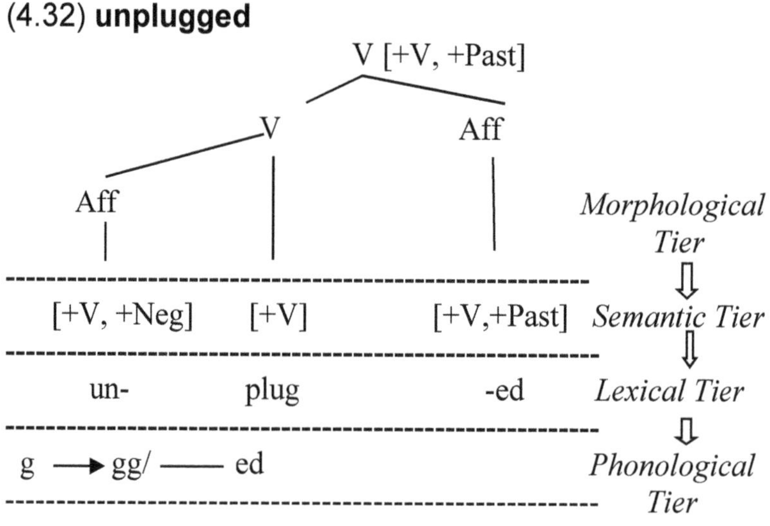

The verb *plug* [+V] is prefixed by *un-* [+V, +Neg] and suffixed by the past morpheme *–ed* [+V, +Past], which is the Head. Phonologically, the last consonant is doubled because it is followed by *–ed.*

(4.33) **cut**

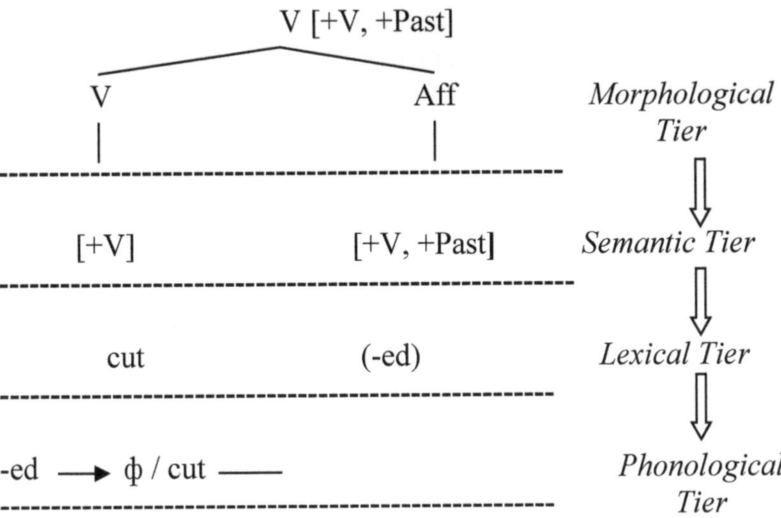

This is a case of zero affixation as *cut* is an irregular verb. Semantically, the past morpheme *–ed* exists even though it is not realised at the phonological level. It is an important element, as it constitutes the Head of the verb.

Concerning the notion of headedness, complex words in English are right-headed in that it is the last suffix on the right which passes its semantic features to the top node.

4.3.2. Lingala complex words

Word formation is very exciting in Bantu Languages as from one root may derive connected nouns and verbs. From the root ***-sal-*** *(work)*, the following words may be derived:

(4.34)

Ko-sal-a	'to work'
Ko-sal-is-an-a	'to help each other'
Ko-sal-el-a	'to work for'
ko-sal-is-a	'to make s.o work/ to hepl"
ko-sal-is-el-a	'to cause to do sth for s.o)
ko-sal-am-a	'to be done'
mu-sal-a	'work/job)
mo-sal-i	'worker'
li-sal-is-i	'help'
e-sal-el-o	'the way of doing/working"
bo-sal-is-as-an-i	'mutual help (one another)

To illustrate the NTS theory, three of the words above will be used.

(4.35) **ko-sal-am-a** ' to be done'

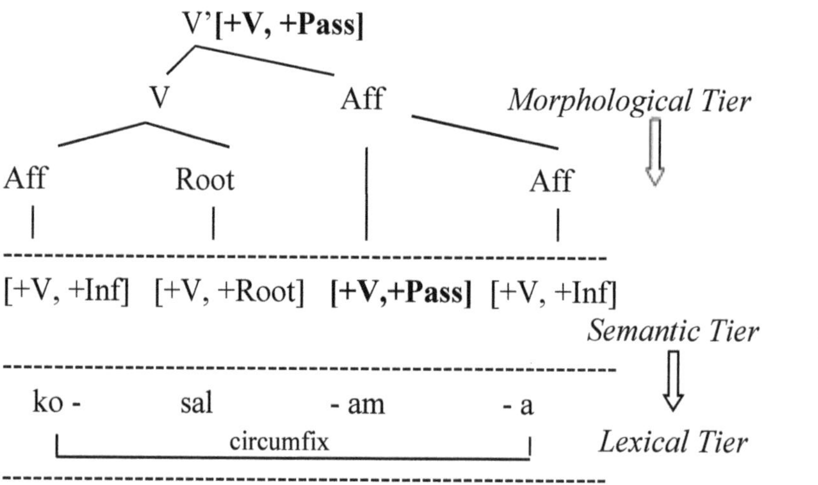

The passive affix *–am-* [+V, +Pass] is the head of the verb of which features are passed up to the top node V. Furthermore, the combination of the affixes *ko-* and *–a* is considered as *circumfix*, as they are added simultaneously to the root to form the infinitive.

(4.36) **ko-sal-is-an-a** 'to help one another'

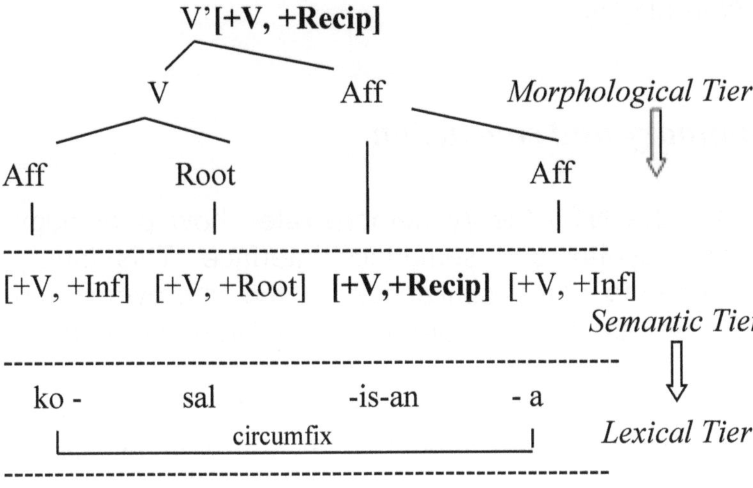

,

The reciprocal *–as-an-* [+V, +Recip] is the Head of the verb.

(4.37) **mo-sal-i** 'worker'

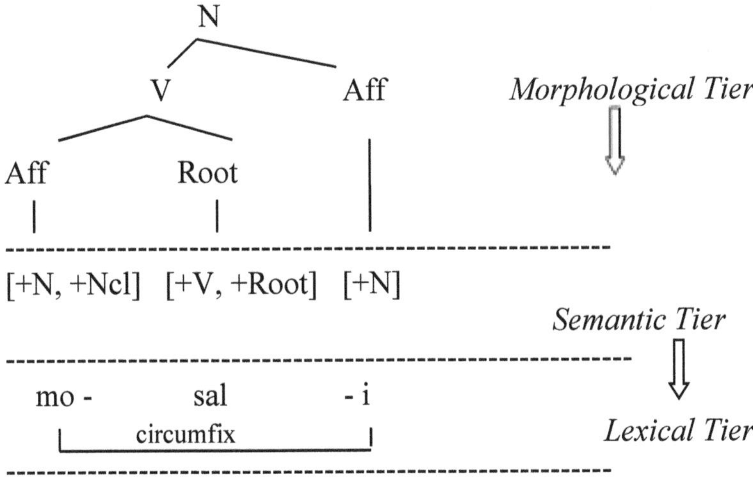

The affixes *mo-* and *–i* are regarded as a round affix, a circumfix, which expresses the 'doer of the action' like the suffix *–er* in English.

4.4. Summary and conclusion

Empirically, the NTS theory demonstrates how phonology, morphology, syntax and semantics interface. This theory, although bearing some similarities, is the improvement of such theories as the Lexical-Functional Grammar and the Auto-Lexical Syntax.
The Auto-Lexical Syntax, developed by Sadock M. Jerrold (1991), suggests a dual representation with respect to rules of morphology and syntax. The representation has two levels: the morphological representation, which is the top tree, and the syntactic representation, the lower tree.

The NTS theory is very explicit when it comes to word structure. It provides morphological components, semantic features, grammatical categories and phonological rules that apply in.
In my NTS theory, I have been inspired by Lieber's (1980, 1984) Morphological Frames and Features Percolation theories, as well Marantz' (1984) Lexical Structures of extended verbs.

CHAPTER 5: GENERAL CONCLUSION

5.1. Summary

The verb in Lingala, as in most Bantu languages, is referred to as verb unit as it is highly agglutinative and complex. The verb base, made of the root and extensions, constitutes the nucleus to which both pre-stem and post-stem affixes are attached. Pre-stem affixes include personal pronouns, noun classes, the future, the progressive and the reflexive. Habitual, perfect, past and present constitute post-stem affixes.
Extensions affect the grammatical argument of the verb by reducing or increasing the valence. The passive extension is valence-reducing, while the applicative and causative extensions increase the valence.

What makes this work unique is the use of generative theories to analyse syntactic affixation. Lieber's Morphological Sub-categorisation Frames provides each bound and free morpheme with a frame that states the category they must attach to, together with their morpho-syntactic features. His Feature Percolation Conventions (FPCs) theory explains the way features of affixes are passed to the dominating node which branches in a word tree diagram.

A far as morphological valence alteration is concerned, Marantz's “merger” theory explains how extension morphemes behave as independent units at the logico-semantic structure of the sentence before 'merging' with the verb root at the s structure.
Using Baker's 'incorporation' theory, I have analysed the way future and reflexive affixes in Lingala function respectively as 'will' and 'oneself' in English at the S-structure with their own nodes. They 'incorporate' with the verb at the D-structure, but leave a trace ***(ei)*** in their previous environment. The same trace is co-indexed in their new environment.

As a contribution, I have developed what is called the N-Tier Structure (NTS) theory, being inspired by the N-Tier Architecture theory used in Software Engineering. Contrary to Marantz who provides two different tree structures (lexical and syntactic), my main idea is that all syntactic, morphological, lexical and phonological information could be displayed on “all-in-one” tree structures with distinct tiers or layers, where 'N' refers to the number of tiers in a structure.
Input sentences derive input tree structures before valence alteration, while output sentences generate output tree structures after valence-decreasing or increasing.
Furthermore, the NTS theory has been applied to English passive transformation and word structure to test its universality.

5.2. Relevance of this paper

This research paper is a further contribution to the structural description of Bantu languages. It is a worthy guide for students as well as researchers in Linguistics. As for Lingala speakers, this work constitutes a foundation to a better understanding of the language structure.

5.3. Further research

The N-Tier Structure theory is still in its embryonic state. Further development of the theory will be carried out with its application to other theoretical aspects of linguistics in different languages.

Bibliography

Baker, Mark. 1988. *Incorporation: A Theory of Grammatical Function Changing*. University of Chicago Press.

Batota-Mpeho, R. 2002. *The Morphology-syntax Interface in Kikongo*, MA Dissertation, Marien Ngouabi University.

Derek Nurse. 2007. *The Emergence of Tense in Early Bantu.* In Selected Proceedings of the 37th Annual Conference on Bantu Linguistics, ed. Doris L. Payne and Jaime El Peňa, 164-179. Sommerville MA: Cascadilla Proceedings Project.

Derek Nurse, Rose, Sarah and Hewson John. *Verbal categories in Niger-Congo Languages.* (With the collaboration from Christa Baudoin-Lietz).

Dixon, R.M.W & Aikhenvald, Alexandra V. 2000. *Changing Valency: Case studies in Transitivity*. CUP.
Marantz, A. 1984. *On the Nature of Grammatical Relation*, Cambridge, MA:MIT.

Fabb, N.1984. *Syntactic Affixation*, Ph.D. Dissertation. MIT.

Guthrie, Malcom. 1948. *The classification of the Bantu Languages*. Oxford University Press.

Hinnebuscu, T. J. 1989. *Bantu in the Niger-Congo Languages.* Edited by John Bendo/ Samuel Lanham. New York – London. University Press of America.

Kay Williamson, R. Blench. 2000. "The Niger-Congo Languages", in Bernd Heine and Derek Nurse (eds), African Languages, map of the Niger-Congo Languages.

Kula, Nancy C and Lutz, Martin. *Argument structure and Agencies in Bemba passives.* University of Essex and SOAS.

Laura Mcpherson. 2008. *Descriptive and theoretical account of Luganda verbal morphology.* Submitted to Scripps College in partial fulfilment of the degree of BA.

Lieber, Rochelle. 1980. *The Organisation of Lexicon*, Ph.D. Dissertation. MIT.
Liber, Rochelle. 1983. *Argument Linking and Compounding in English*, Linguistic Inquiry (LI) 14, 251-86.

Lyons, John. 1968. *Introduction to theoretical Linguistics*, Cambridge: CUP.

Payne, Thomas E. 2006. *Exploring Language Structure: A student guide*, CUP.

Sadock M. Jerrold. 1991. *A theory of parallel grammatical representation.* The University Press of Chicago.

Samba-Samba, Philippe. 1990. *The System of Tone in Kikongo*, Ph.D. Dissertation, Lancaster University.

Samba-Samba, Philippe .2000. *The Grammar of Extension in Kikongo*, a research paper, Marien Ngouabi University

Spencer, Andrew. 1991. *Morphological Theory: an introduction to word structure in generative grammar*, Basil Blackwell, CUP.

Trithart, Lee. 1979. *Topicality to the relational view in Bantu passive*, UCLA Studies in African Linguistics, Volume 10.

Walter de Gruyter,1989. *Status and functions of Languages and Language varieties,* Ulrich Ammon, International Sociological Association.

Appendix

Appendix1. Table of conjugation in Lingala

ф= omitted personal pronoun

Present na-bin-**í** I-dance-**Pres** (I just danced= recent past)	**Present perfect** na-bin-**ak-í** I-dance-**Perf-Pres** (I have danced)
Past na-bin-**á** I-dance-**Past** (I danced)	**Past Perfect** na-bin-**ak-á** I-dance-**Perf-Past** (I had danced)
Future simple na-**kó**-bin-a I-**Fut**-dance-FV (I will dance)	**Future Perfect** na-**kó**-bin-**ak**-a I-**Fut**-dance-**Perf**-FV (I will have danced)
Present Progressive na-zal-í ko-bin-a I-be-Pres Inf-dance-FV (I am dancing)	**Present Perfect Progressive** na-zal-**ak-í** ko-bin-a I-be-**Perf-Pres** Inf-dance-FV (I have been dancing)
Past Progressive na-zal-á ko-bin-a I-be-Past Inf-dance-FV (I was dancing)	**Past Perfect Progressive** na-zal-**ak-á** ko-bin-a I-be-**Perf-Past** Inf-dance-FV (I had been dancing)

<table>
<tr><td>Imperative

ɸ -bín-a
2sg-dance-Fv
(dance)

to- bín-a
1pl-dance-Fv
(Let us dance)

bo-bín-a
2pl-dance-Fv
(Let you dance)</td><td>Future Subjunctive

na-kó-zal-a ko-zal-a
1sg-Fut-be-Fv Inf-be-Fv
(I were to be)</td></tr>
<tr><td>Present Subjunctive

ná-zal-a
1sg-be-Fv
(I be)</td><td>Perfect Subjunctive

ná-zal-ak-a
1sg-be-Perf-Fv
(I were)</td></tr>
<tr><td></td><td></td></tr>
</table>

Appendix 2: Maps of Niger-Congo Languages

From Kay Williamson, R. Blench. 2000. "The Niger-Congo Languages", in Bernd Heine and Derek Nurse (editions), African Languages, map of the Niger-Congo Languages (p.12).

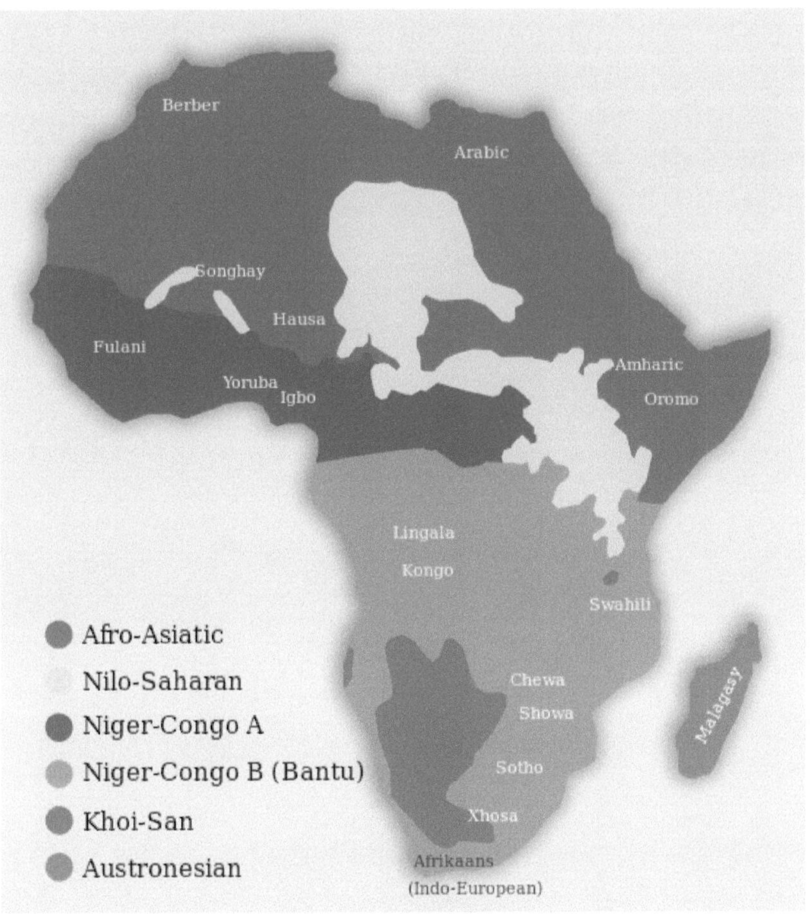

Map showing the approximate distribution of Bantu vs. other Niger–Congo languages (Source: Wikipedia).

www.ingramcontent.com/pod-product-compliance
Ingram Content Group UK Ltd.
Pitfield, Milton Keynes, MK11 3LW, UK
UKHW041930190726
13854UKWH00004B/1534